CHARTING
THE FUTURE

CHARTING
THE FUTURE

THE READER'S DIGEST ASSOCIATION, INC.
Pleasantville, New York/Montreal

Quest for the Unknown
Created, edited, and designed by DK Direct Limited

A DORLING KINDERSLEY BOOK

DK DIRECT LIMITED

Senior Editor Richard Williams
Editor Deirdre Headon
Editorial Research Julie Whitaker
Editorial Secretary Pat White

Senior Art Editor Simon Webb
Art Editor Mark Osborne
Picture Research Frances Vargo; **Picture Assistant** Sharon Southren

Editorial Director Jonathan Reed; **Design Director** Ed Day
Production Manager Ian Paton

Volume Consultant Brian Innes
Contributors Barry Fantoni, Fred Gettings, Reg Grant, Stuart R. Kaplan,
Francis X. King, Roy Stemman

Illustrators Roy Flooks, Matthew Richardson
Photographers Martin Eidemak,
Simon Farnhell, Andrew Griffin, Mark Hamilton, Imago,
Steve Lyne, Susanna Price, Alex Wilson

Library of Congress Cataloging in Publication Data

Charting the future.
     p.   cm. — (Quest for the unknown)
"A Dorling Kindersley book."
Includes index.
ISBN 0-89577-441-0
   1. Divination.   2. Fortune-telling.   3. Divination—History.
4. Fortune-telling—History.   I. Reader's Digest Association.
II.   Series.
BF1751. C42 1992
133. 3—dc20   92-8818

Printed in the United States of America

FOREWORD

*A*nthropologists have suggested that the instinct and ability of primitive humankind to look ahead gave us a distinct advantage over other animals in the struggle for survival in the dawn of our history. To this day, trying to find out what the future holds remains something of an obsession with our species.

Over thousands of years, we have devised hundreds of divinatory systems. The techniques have included calculating planetary positions, studying fires, dealing cards, rolling dice, flipping coins, reading palms, examining animals' entrails, and watching the flight of birds. Prophets, fortune-tellers, and soothsayers have always been on hand to offer advice about the future; from the destiny of a nation to that of the humblest peasant in the land.

This volume examines the history of divination, and the theories behind the most popular methods. It analyzes the techniques most commonly employed today. It shows the reader how the various methods are used, and how the results are interpreted.

Do any of these techniques work? This has not been proved. There are many examples of both accurate and inaccurate prediction in these pages. Certainly some people seem to have a gift for divination. This could be the instinct of our primitive forebears, well-developed by evolution. On the other hand, it may be merely a well-disguised skill at picking up clues from the past and the present, and using them intelligently to guess what will happen next. Whether it's a matter of luck, skill, or instinct, this book contains all you need to know in order to discover if you too have the power to chart the future.

— The Editors

CONTENTS

A LIFE FORETOLD

Is every individual's destiny set out in the stars from the moment of birth? Many people fervently believe so, and many more half-seriously consult their horoscope every day in the newspaper. We hired an experienced astrologer to help us put this theory to the test.

We asked our astrologer to draw up the birth chart for a mystery person. He was told only that the subject was a woman born on November 12, 1929, at 5:31 A.M. in Philadelphia, Pennsylvania. In the following pages the astrologer describes how he drew up the horoscope, and interpreted it to map out the course of the woman's life. (For more detail on the astrological terms, and the techniques used to draw up your own horoscope, turn to Chapter Two: "The Cosmic Clock.")

> "People with Venus in Libra are always physically attractive; their sex-drive is intense, and as a result they tend to marry young. Being good-looking people, they have little difficulty in finding a congenial partner."

THE HOROSCOPE

Subject: female
Born: 5:31 A.M., November 12, 1929
Location: Philadelphia, Pennsylvania;
*   longitude 75 degrees west*

❝I converted the subject's birth time into its equivalent sidereal time of 8:55. Having established this, I erected the midheaven at 12 degrees Leo (at the top of the chart). I am working with the simplified Equal House system here, so that puts the eastern horizon, or ascendant – the sign of the zodiac that is rising over the horizon at the moment of birth – at 12 degrees Scorpio (on the left-hand side of the chart). This means that the division of each house will fall at 12 degrees of the appropriate sign. As you can see from the chart on the opposite page – and as you would expect at this hour of a winter morning – the sun will not rise for another two hours or so, and it's at 20 degrees Scorpio, below the horizon.

"The sign of the zodiac that is ascendant will govern the basic physical characteristics of the subject. Scorpio indicates that this woman is strong, of average stature, with thick, generally curling, hair; her face may be inclined to squareness, with a sharp nose. Scorpios are usually strong and healthy, with good resistance to disease.

Rising sun and setting moon
"The sun in Scorpio gives us a first glimpse of what the subject's nature may be. Scorpios are generally extremely powerful personalities, calm and watchful, with an almost hypnotic intensity about them. Although strong-willed and sometimes apparently withdrawn, Scorpios are at the same time deeply sensitive. The position of the sun in the ascendant house means that all these personality traits are likely to be enhanced in the character.

"In this birth chart the moon has set, and is well below the horizon at 17 degrees Pisces. This tells us that our subject is like a 'psychic sponge,' soaking up the thoughts and emotions of others. In consequence she is easily hurt, and often feels vulnerable. At such times she is likely to withdraw into herself.

The morning stars
"The planets Venus and Mercury are morning stars in this horoscope, rising ahead of the Sun: Mercury is at 10 degrees Scorpio on the horizon, and Venus is even higher in the sky at 28 degrees Libra.

"Mercury in Scorpio tells us that the subject has an acutely penetrating intellect that is capable of profound insights. Venus governs the sign of Libra. In this birth chart, Venus appears in her own house, at 28 degrees Libra, and therefore her influence is particularly strong. People with Venus in Libra are always physically attractive; their sex-drive is intense, and as a result they tend to marry young. Being good-looking people, they have little difficulty in finding a congenial partner.

"People born with Venus in Libra thrive in the social environment because they display an innate understanding of other people's feelings. This may sometimes be in conflict with the Scorpian side of this woman's nature, which is more withdrawn.

"Now Mars, we find, is very close to the Sun, almost in conjunction, and in his own house at 26 degrees Scorpio. Scorpio is often taken as the symbol of sex, and here we have two powerful and masculine planets – one of them in the sign of his rulership, and both in the ascendant. The powerful sex-drive implied here may cause problems.

Far-flung planets
"We now come to the planets that are much farther from the earth. Jupiter, which falls in Gemini, is said to be 'in detriment' – that is, directly opposite his ruling house of Sagittarius – and, as you can see, Jupiter is also in opposition to Saturn, which is usually regarded as a

bad influence. Jupiter is also 'retrograde' (that is, it appears to be going in the opposite direction to the other planets). This suggests that the inquiring mind represented by Gemini won't be tempered by the maturity of Jupiter. This person is likely to explore many subjects – but only superficially.

The planet Uranus spends about seven years in each sign of the zodiac, and all those born in the years 1928–34 have this planet in Aries. These people reveal the typical effect of Aries – impulsiveness combined with creativity – in their enthusiasm for and ability to adapt to new lifestyles. However, in this horoscope Uranus too is retrograde as if trying to return to Pisces. This creates conflict, as Pisceans yearn for the past.

Domestic concerns

"Finally, let's take a look at the positions of the most distant planets, Neptune and Pluto. They are both high in the midheaven at the moment of birth. Neptune is in detriment in Virgo, and exerts a limiting influence on a horoscope that is otherwise strong in creativity. The planet Pluto in Cancer – a sign concerned very much with personal emotions and domestic concerns – will bring a degree of uncertainty to these matters.

Heavenly aspects

"The next stage in interpretation is to look at the positions of the planets in relation to one another – their 'aspects' – and to the 12 houses of the horoscope. (The 12 houses follow the 12 divisions of the horoscope; they are numbered counterclockwise from the ascendant sign, which falls in the first house.) Although there are some encouraging indications, I am not happy about the overall look of this horoscope. The Sun and Mars are nearly in conjunction in the first house. This part of the horoscope represents the subject herself: her character, her behavior in general and how she relates to others. A conjunction is what is known as a 'harmonious' aspect, and here it indicates many good things: vitality, good health, courage, initiative, and the ability to lead others. All these positive traits are only slightly modified by a tendency to be rather quick-tempered. However, I've already mentioned the strong sexual indications for this house, and would predict a certain amount of trouble in the subject's love life.

A discordant aspect

"In the second house, Saturn is in opposition to Jupiter in the eighth house, which is a 'discordant' aspect. Taking the position of these two planets together, I get the feeling that there will be sadness and misfortune in the subject's life, and perhaps more than one unexpected death. Money will come by marriage, but a death may result in a reduction in finances, creating the need (or at least the impulse) for the subject to take up work relatively late in her life. The Moon is in the fifth house, and is described as being 'in trine,' that is, positioned at the points of a triangle — a harmonious aspect — to the Sun and Mars. However, the Moon is square — a discordant aspect — to Jupiter and Saturn. The fifth house governs family life, marriage, and children. I would expect the subject to have several children, but her chart indicates a degree of uncertainty in their development because of the presence of Uranus in the same house. When combined with the bad aspect of the Moon to Jupiter and Saturn, I can see family quarrels and disappointments in this woman's life. Pluto and Neptune in the ninth and tenth houses respectively suggest uncertainty in travel and the possibility of relationships with foreigners. There is

> **"Pluto and Neptune in the ninth and tenth houses suggest uncertainty in travel and the possibility of relationships with foreigners."**

also an indication that the subject may take up a prominent position in public life. In these two fields there is likely to be considerable disruption at some stage in her life. Pluto is square to Virgo, again indicating unhappiness in love, which is further shown by Neptune being square to Mars. This latter discordant aspect is also traditionally connected with some kind of trouble with drugs or alcohol.

"The twelfth house represents the inner psychic life, and the indications here are not good. Mercury suggests that there will be many worries, and the presence of Venus implies that they may well be concerned with the discovery of secret love affairs. The position of the Sun, Moon and Pluto in trine, and the same relationship between Saturn and Neptune suggest that the subject may have a strong interest in psychic matters, and possibly even some psychic powers herself.

Summing-up

"How would I sum up this horoscope? If I had drawn it up at the time of birth, I would have said that this baby girl is going to grow up into an outstandingly beautiful woman, probably dark-haired, with fine eyes and an upright carriage. But for all her beauty she will have a cool, withdrawn nature. She will marry, perhaps more than once, and have several children. But she will not have a happy married life: there will be misfortune, problems with the children, sudden death, troubles in love.

"This birth chart indicates a strong and indomitable woman. Her creative gifts fit her for a career in one of the media. Later in life she may show a tendency to withdraw into herself, living in her dreams and memories, and seeking comfort in the psychic world."

13

BIOGRAPHY OF PRINCESS GRACE OF MONACO (1929–82)

Grace Kelly was born on November 12, 1929, in Philadelphia. She was the third of four children born to Irish/American self-made millionaire John Kelly and his German-immigrant wife, Margaret Majer.

The Kelly gang

Grace was raised in an affluent neighborhood. It was a disciplined yet lively household. John Kelly was a busy man, with a roving eye, and spent little time at home. But his vivacity and love of practical jokes contrasted strongly with his wife's somewhat dour and rigid approach to raising a family.

According to her mother: "There was always something a bit different, a bit withdrawn about Grace. She was a frail little girl and sickly a good deal of the time, very susceptible to colds. She was completely self-sufficient and could amuse herself for hours by making up little plays with her dolls."

Grace nurtured a desire to be an actress from a very early age, possibly influenced by the fact that her father's brother, George Kelly, was a successful playwright. She auditioned for the American Academy of Dramatic Arts in New York City and started her training in the fall of 1947.

A budding actress

Grace was a beautiful and immaculately groomed young woman. When there was a lack of straight acting work, she took on modeling assignments. This led to television work, and then to movies. Grace landed her first film role in *High Noon* (1953) playing Gary Cooper's young bride. She was then 24 years old.

Grace's rise to major movie stardom was meteoric. To list her films is to list some of the best-remembered movies of the 1950's: *Mogambo* with Clark Gable; *Dial M for Murder* with Ray Milland; *The Country Girl* with Bing Crosby (for which Grace won an Oscar); *Rear Window* with James Stewart; *High Society* with Frank Sinatra, and *To Catch a Thief* with Cary Grant. In all the movies she appeared in, Grace had a style all her own, coming across as a cool, untouchable beauty.

The Year of Grace

In 1955 *Life* magazine published Grace's photograph on the cover, calling it "The Year of Grace." Gossip columnists speculated wildly about her alleged love affairs with Hollywood's major stars: Clark Gable, Bing Crosby, William Holden, and Ray Milland. In the spring of 1955 she went to the Cannes Film Festival in the south of France. There she met Prince Rainier of the Grimaldi family, the ruler of the tiny principality of Monaco.

In January 1956, Grace's engagement to Prince Rainier was announced. On April 19, 1956, Grace became Her Serene Highness, Princess Grace of Monaco – in a wedding dress designed by the costume department of Metro-Goldwyn-Meyer Studios. In the best movie tradition, it was a fairy tale come true.

The world's favorite princess

Grace immediately became the world's favorite princess, playing the role to perfection. She had three children: Caroline, Albert, and a few years later, Stephanie. She was a devoted mother.

When these children reached adolescence they proved themselves to be as strong-willed as Grace had been in her struggle to be an actress. Princess Caroline, in particular, caused her parents considerable anxiety when she insisted on marrying French socialite Philippe Junot in 1978 – the marriage lasted only two years. Some time later, in 1990, a major tragedy struck the family when Caroline's second husband, Stefano Casiraghi, was killed in a powerboat accident.

Despite numerous offers, Princess Grace never returned to Hollywood. She appeared content to pursue her other roles as wife and mother, and as princess of Monaco. She died in 1982 in a tragic car accident in the south of France.

COMMENT

At first sight the horoscope appears surprisingly accurate. There are many statements that can easily be applied to Princess Grace. The astrologer mentions beauty, sensitivity, a withdrawn nature, a career in one of the media. There are also references to travel, relationships with foreigners, and public position. Problems with children and unexpected death are also forecast.

All these indications may well be right there in the birth chart. But look at it from the astrologer's point of view for a moment. He is asked to produce a birth chart for a mystery woman for a book. Obviously the person is going to be someone famous, so that the reader will have some idea of her life, and therefore of the accuracy of the reading.

An educated guess?

Now look back at the list of what we took to be correct predictions in the first graph. Take any woman born in the late 1920's who is well-known enough for her life to be common property. She has to be in a prominent public position, first of all. She is likely to be attractive. She is almost bound to be involved in one of the media, and as such is likely to be perceived as sensitive. Since she is in the public eye, she is quite likely to be seen as withdrawn in private life. She is also certain to have traveled abroad, and to have been romantically linked with at least one foreigner. Everyone has problems with their children. And death is nearly always unexpected.

In short, the astrologer's hits, although disguised, are predictable. And there are quite a few misses. The astrologer

thought the mystery subject was dark-haired, and of average height. He said that Scorpios are usually healthy – but Grace was a sickly child. He thought that a sudden death would cause her financial worries.

Mistaken identity

After he had completed the chart, we asked the astrologer to take a guess at the identity of the mystery subject. He said that he suspected it was Jackie Kennedy, *née* Bouvier, later Onassis. She too was born in the eastern U.S. in 1929. Reading the horoscope again in the light of this, all the pieces fall into place. The horoscope that we originally thought applied to Princess Grace now applies equally well, or slightly better, to someone else altogether. It appears that we try to fit the fortune being told to the person we know it's meant for.

This illustrates how heavily all types of divination rely on how we interpret the messages we receive about the future – the writing on the wall is rarely in plain English.

There seems to be a desire in the human psyche to believe in methods of predicting the future. This is something we must bear in mind throughout this volume. There is a fine line between what may be achieved by true divination or clairvoyance (if such a thing does, in fact, exist), and what may be achieved by the combination of human skill, intuition, and a little bit of luck. In our quest for the unknown – in this case, a genuine divinatory method and a sensitive system of interpretation – we should not allow ourselves to be gullible.

> The horoscope that we originally thought applied to Princess Grace now applies equally well, or slightly better, to someone else altogether. It appears that we try to fit the fortune being told to the person we know it's meant for.

HIT:
Personality
The astrologer says that Scorpios have: "...very powerful personalities, calm and watchful, with an almost hypnotic intensity about them....Although strong-willed and sometimes apparently withdrawn, Scorpios are...deeply sensitive." Grace was a quiet, determined child, and her characteristic quality on screen was her cool, hypnotic intensity.

MISS:
Physical characteristics
The horoscope describes a subject with dark, curly hair and of average height. Grace had straight blonde hair and was taller than average at 5 feet 7 inches.

HIT:
Travel and foreigners
The astrologer suggests: "uncertainty in travel and the possibility of relationships with foreigners....the subject may take up a prominent position in public life." This is accurate on all counts.

MISS:
Money matters
The horoscope mentions a sudden death that may cause a reduction in finances, causing Grace to take up work late in life. The first sudden death in the family was that of Grace herself.

HIT:
Unexpected death
"There will be...perhaps more than one unexpected death." Two sudden deaths occurred in the Grimaldi family: the first of Grace herself, the second of Princess Caroline's second husband.

CHAPTER ONE

THE NATURE OF TIME

Any attempt to predict the future must acknowledge its relationship with the present and the past. Time as a circle, time as an arrow — these are just two of the theories that have been proposed over the centuries to explain the puzzling nature of time.

Most people feel they know instinctively what time is, because they experience it in every instant of their lives. Yet they might be at a loss to describe or explain it.

If ordinary people think about time at all, they probably visualize it as a stream or a river, flowing swiftly from the past into the future. It is generally seen as irreversible and unrepeatable — a one-way street with no U-turns and no stopping allowed, leading straight into an uncertain future.

But in earlier civilizations a different view of time often prevailed. Perhaps

Mayan calendar
This page from the Dresden Codex contains elaborate astronomical calculations. It is one of the few remaining fragments of an impressive store of knowledge compiled by the Mayas and destroyed by the invading Spaniards in the 15th century.

> "If you ask me what time is, I don't know the answer. If you don't ask me, I do."
> **St. Augustine**

because they had no clocks and were in tune with the great rhythms of the natural world — the progression of the seasons, the waxing and waning of the moon — these civilizations tended to see time as circular and repetitive.

A cycle of universes
According to the Brahman cosmology of ancient India, for instance, there was not one universe, but a cycle of universes, being born and dying in endless succession. Each universe flourished for one day in the life of the creator-god, Brahma, which was equivalent to 4,320,000,000 human years. Then the universe faded for one Brahma night.

As transient as soap bubbles on the surface of eternity, these universes would appear and disappear for 100 Brahma years, but even then the process would not end. Other gods would take

over, and so the cycle of creation and destruction would continue.

The Mayas, who were at the height of their power in Central America between A.D. 600 and 900, were meticulous students of time. They produced a calendar more accurate than the one used today — it was out of alignment by only two days every 10,000 years. Our Gregorian calendar, on the other hand, needs adjusting by three days over a similar period.

Time as a relay race
The Mayan concept of the nature of time, however, may seem bizarre to us. The Mayas believed that each period of time — each day, month, and year — was a burden carried by a god along the road to eternity. Time was a sort of relay race, repeating itself in 52-year cycles, as the same gods once again took up their burden. Events did not repeat themselves exactly as before but followed a predictable pattern, since similar happenings would recur when the same god carried the day.

Some ancient Greek philosophers took an extreme view of the circular recurrence of time. Pythagoras and his followers believed in an exact repetition of all events as the cycle of time came around once more.

It was the spread of Christianity that replaced this cyclical view of time with that of a straight progression from the past into the future. In an adaptation of existing Judaic philosophy, Christianity popularized the belief that Christ had come to earth to save humankind once only, at a precise moment in history. At an unknown but equally precise moment in the future, there would come the Last

St. Augustine

Judgment, another once-and-for-all historical event. So time had to be a fixed one-way path, although Christian mystics were sometimes blessed with a fleeting vision of eternity or "the world beyond time."

Traces of the older, cyclical view of time persisted, however, until the scientific revolution of the 17th century seemed to consign such a concept to the dustbin of history. The time recognized by the new science of Newton and Galileo was linear time — a straight line stretching from birth to death.

Clock time

The widespread use of clocks quickly led to a general acceptance of the new scientific concept of time. People believed that the flow of time was objectively the same for everyone and could be measured by the regular ticking of a timepiece. In the words of 17th-century mathematician Isaac Barrow: "Whether we move or are still, whether we sleep or wake, Time pursues the even tenor of its way."

The highly successful civilization of the modern scientific and industrial age was built upon this concept of clock time. From train timetables to working hours to the precise scheduling of radio and TV programs, modern life is

Hindu reincarnation
Hinduism embodies in its doctrine of reincarnation a cyclical view of time. This 18th-century painting of the Hindu god Vishnu and his 10 avatars, or incarnations, is from the Jaipur area in India.

governed by the ticking of the clock. Yet 20th-century science has thrown this concept of linear time into disarray. Since Albert Einstein published the first of his relativity theories in 1905, scientists have had to cope with an idea of time that seems to defy common sense. According to Einstein, time is not the same for everyone "whether we

From cradle to grave
This portrait of Sir Henry Unton painted in 1596 demonstrates the Western view of life and death. Sir Henry's birth is illustrated on the right, and his life's path wends across the painting to his funeral on the far left.

Aging and death
This early-16th-century painting by Hans Baldung Grien is entitled "The Ages of Man and Death." Memento mori (a reminder of mortality) was a popular theme in Renaissance art. Its motivation was religious, since it acted as a warning of the transitory nature of life and the vanity of earthly pride and pleasures.

move or are still." He demonstrated that everything about time finally depends on your point of view.

For instance, can we tell exactly when a particular event — say, the explosion of a star — took place? An astronomer watching from the planet Zig 100 light years away will see the blinding light of the supernova a full century before an astronomer twice the distance away on the planet Zag. (See Figure 1 below.) So the astronomer on Zig would believe that it happened in, say, A.D. 1800, and the astronomer on Zag would date it at A.D. 1900. Both opinions would be correct, from a subjective point of view. Neither of the two observers would give the "right" or "wrong" date for the explosion — both points of view would be valid.

Now suppose two supernovas explode and the flashes of both can be seen by our two astronomers. Can we tell if the two explosions happened at exactly the same time? It appears that we cannot. Depending on their positions relative to the two stars, the two observers might

even disagree over which exploded first. On Zig it may seem that supernova A exploded before supernova B, while on Zag the explosion of B was seen years earlier than A. (See Figure 2 below.)

Thus, depending on the point of view, one person's future might be considered another person's past. If no two events can ever be said to have happened at precisely the same time, it makes no sense at all to talk of the present. As Einstein wrote: "The distinction between past, present, and future is an illusion."

Time stood still?

As soon as people cease being stationary and start to move through Einstein's universe, the consequences become very strange indeed. According to relativity theory — and it has been confirmed by practical experiments — when you accelerate, for example when taking off in an airplane, your watch goes slightly slower than the clock in the airport lounge you have just left. This effect is so small as to be almost undetectable at normal airspeeds, but it can be measured at the extreme speeds involved in space travel.

To cope with this warping of time in the universe, Einstein devised the notion of "spacetime." In spacetime, Einstein suggested, time was a dimension like height, breadth, or length. Every event or object could be situated at a point defined by the three dimensions of space and the "fourth dimension" of

POINTS OF VIEW

These diagrams illustrate that everything about time depends in the end on your point of view. In Figure 1, the astronomer on planet Zig will see the supernova 100 years before the astronomer on planet Zag. In Figure 2, the astronomer on planet Zig will believe supernova A exploded 100 years before supernova B; the astronomer on planet Zag will believe the reverse is true.

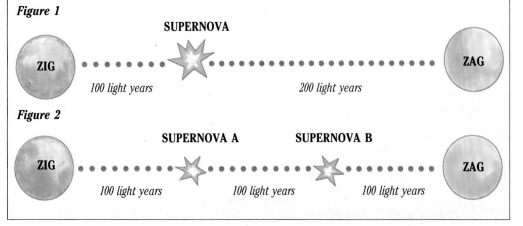

Figure 1

SUPERNOVA

ZIG · · · · · · · · · · ⭐ · · · · · · · · · · · · · · · ZAG

100 light years   *200 light years*

Figure 2

SUPERNOVA A   SUPERNOVA B

ZIG · · · · · · · ⭐ · · · · · · · ⭐ · · · · · · · ZAG

100 light years   *100 light years*   *100 light years*

EINSTEIN AND THE ASTRONAUTS

According to Einstein's relativity theories, the speed at which time passes is affected by relative acceleration. For instance, if a rocket in the form of a giant illuminated clock was blasted off into space at extremely high speed, observers on earth looking at the clock face rising into the night sky would see it ticking over the minutes more slowly than the watches on their wrists. But the crew of the rocket would see the rocket clock keeping the same time as their wristwatches — because they would be accelerating at the same speed.

This has weird implications for future space travel. Imagine that it is the year 2100 and scientists can now propel spaceships at speeds that make exploration beyond our solar system a practical project. When an astronaut says farewell to his family, he is 30 years old and his wife is 26. They have two children aged 4 and 6.

In this hypothetical example, the astronaut blasts off into space for a long round trip to another part of the galaxy, traveling at half the speed of light. He celebrates Christmas in space five times during the voyage. He is 35 years old when he returns to earth.

Albert Einstein

But back home, the clocks have been running faster and far more time has passed. The astronaut's family have been missing him for ten years. His wife is 36 years old. Resuming their relationship requires some readjustment, since she is now both chronologically and physiologically older than her husband, instead of younger. The astronaut's children are now 14 and 16. Theoretically, if he had traveled any longer or faster, he might have come home to find that not only his wife, but his children too, were older than him.

If the crew of a spaceship could travel through space faster than the speed of light, then from the point of view of an observer on earth they would seem to head backward through time into the past. In theory, the astronauts could arrive back from their journey younger than when they left. However, according to Einstein's theories, the speed of light is the fastest speed that can exist; therefore no spaceship could ever break the light barrier, and this form of time travel could never happen.

time. Just as a house, for instance, spreads out in three directions, front to back, top to bottom, and side to side, so it also stretches back through the fourth dimension to the time when it was built, and forward to its future destruction.

In the mind of Einstein, time appeared to become a static, if pliable, part of geometry. If time is a fourth dimension, added on to the three dimensions of space, then it may be wrong to say that time flows or passes. In this case the "passage of time" is an illusion created by the human mind — in the same way that a landscape appears to move past us when we watch it from a car window. In reality, it is our consciousness that moves along the dimension of time.

Radical concepts of time

With the emergence of quantum physics and the detailed study of the behavior of minute subatomic particles, radical concepts of time looked even more appealing. According to some interpretations of quantum theory, there is no place for linear time in it at all. Some subatomic particles regularly move from the future into the past instead of from the past into the future.

Yet quantum physics and relativity are not the whole story. In many areas, "time's arrow" still points clearly from the past into the future along the one-way street.

Long road to chaos

In the familiar nursery rhyme "Humpty Dumpty" the egg-man fell off a wall and broke. "All the king's horses and all the king's men" could not reassemble him. This illustrates the second law of thermodynamics: disorder, or entropy, as it is called, will always increase through time. In the long run all eggs are broken. Time runs in one direction, from order to disorder.

The difficulty in grasping the nature of time is perhaps that we are so totally immersed in it. A fish in the ocean might have a similar problem grasping the nature of water. As writer J. B. Priestley put it: "Pursuing Time, we are like a knight on a quest, condemned to wander through innumerable forests, bewildered and baffled, because the magic beast he is looking for is the horse he is riding."

Time by the sun
This elaborate sundial dates from the late 18th century. When it was made, reliable mechanical clocks had been around for centuries, but there was still a demand for more traditional designs that were operated directly by the movements of the earth and sun.

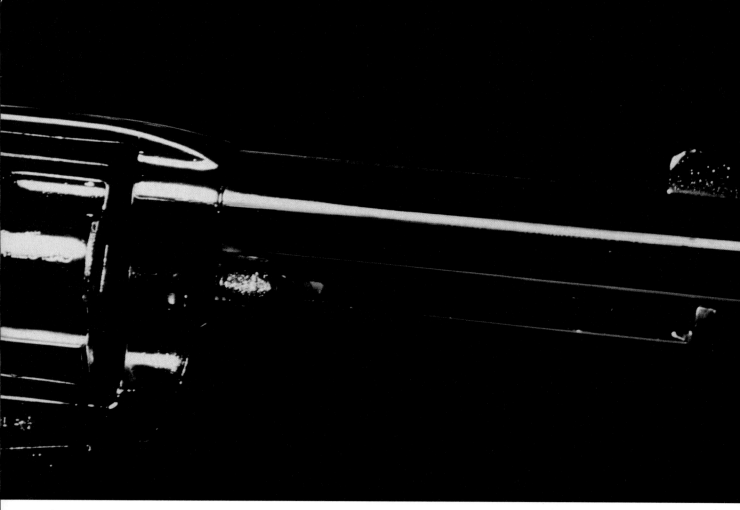

CAN WE KNOW THE FUTURE?

Many attempts have been made to forecast the future by looking at the trends of past and present. Some visionaries even claim to have glimpsed the future exactly as it subsequently occurred.

*I*N THE FALL OF 1913, British dream researcher J. W. Dunne told his sister that he had dreamed of a serious accident. In his dream a train had crashed over an embankment just north of the Forth bridge in Scotland. Dunne had the impression that this crash was going to happen the following spring. On April 14, 1914, about 15 miles north of the Firth of Forth, the famous *Flying Scotsman* mail train plunged off the track onto a golf course 20 feet below. Dunne had apparently foreseen the future. But how could such a thing be possible?

It is certainly possible to know the past directly: not through finding out about it in books or trusting to memories but by seeing it with our own eyes. We only have to stare up into the sky on a clear night. When we look at any star, we are seeing the past, since the light from

Fatal crash
This contemporary news photograph records the scene of the Scottish railway accident foreseen by J. W. Dunne.

An astronomer in a distant galaxy, armed with a powerful telescope, could at this moment be watching the building of the Egyptian pyramids.

that star has taken hundreds of years to reach us. Indeed, the star that we can see twinkling in the darkness of space may no longer exist. In the same way, in theory at least, an astronomer on a planet in a distant galaxy, armed with a powerful telescope, could at this moment be watching the building of the Egyptian pyramids.

But gaining direct knowledge of the future poses quite different problems. You cannot see something that does not exist. And according to the common-sense view of time by which we order most of our lives, the future is a blank, a nonexistent void that will eventually be filled in by the progression of time. From this viewpoint, the only way to predict the future is to study events in the past or the present and make an informed guess about where they will lead. If I see a glass falling off a shelf, I can make a prediction that it will break when it hits the ground. This is predicting the future, even if it is not very impressive.

Types of prediction

Some methods of charting the future, such as astrology and the *I Ching*, claim only to predict what is likely to happen. They make an attempt to perceive the general tendency of events and the shape of an individual's destiny. Their practitioners are like expert chartmakers, trying to show us a passage through the reefs and shoals of life's oceans.

But people such as Dunne, and many prophets, oracles, and seers through the ages, have claimed to have direct

If some people truly can see the future, then the future must already exist.

knowledge of the future. A person who has a premonitory dream — a dream that is later confirmed to have exactly corresponded to an event at some time in the future — has not merely made a prediction. Discounting coincidence, he or she, it would appear, has actually "seen" the future. There is evidence that some premonitions and visions are reliable indicators of the future, yet they pose a severe challenge to our notion of time. For if some people truly can see the future, it seems logical to suggest that the future must already exist.

One way of explaining the idea is by imagining time as a moving picture

Telling the future
This photograph, taken with special equipment, has frozen a moment in time. We have no difficulty in predicting what will happen next. Seeing the future is not so easy in the more complex context of human life.

A hundred years ago the notion of foreseeing the future flew in the face of science, but scientific attitudes toward time have now become strange enough to accommodate this possibility.

being projected onto a screen in front of us. We in the audience have no way of knowing what the next reel will show, yet the whole film is lying in the projection room, complete up to the final frame. If someone could get a peek at it, he could tell us what we were going to see an hour later. In this highly theoretical concept of time the future is, of course, predetermined. We cannot alter what is to happen in the film; we can only sit and watch.

Alternative times
Believers in the paranormal have always been asked to explain why the future should be revealed only in special states — dream sleep or some form of trance. A host of theoretical ideas has been advanced in an effort to account for this. Dunne himself developed an elaborate system in which there were a series of alternative types of time. In the time accessible to our waking self, the future was hidden, but another time accessible to our dream self might allow us to see the future, or at least one of the possible alternative futures.

The eminent psychical researcher H. F. Saltmarsh started by asking the mind-bending question: How long is the present? Saltmarsh put forward the idea that the present moment, of which we are directly conscious, always has a certain duration, even if only a very short one. He suggested that for the unconscious mind, the present might be much longer, stretching well into the future. In dreams and other special states, we might become aware of this longer present time and so have visions of what, to our normal waking sense, would be the future.

A hundred years ago it would have seemed that the notion of foreseeing the future flew in the face of science, but scientific attitudes toward time in the 20th century have become strange enough to accommodate this possibility.

In his book *The Emperor's New Mind* (1989), the mathematician Professor Roger Penrose created a sci-fi scenario based on Einstein's relativity theories that shows how confused science now is about past, present, and future.

Future confusion
In Penrose's example, the rulers of Andromeda, 12 billion miles from our galaxy, are debating whether to dispatch

their intergalactic space fleet to totally annihilate the earth. Earthling observers on various planets in Andromeda's vicinity await the decision with interest. But, depending on their distance from Andromeda, they witness events there at different times. As one concerned citizen follows the debate within the galactic council, a second citizen, on a nearer planet, sees the space fleet set off on its mission. At that point, Penrose writes: "According to one of them the decision lay in the uncertain future, while to the other it lay in the certain past." From the point of view of the first citizen, the second is seeing the future.

Quantum physics

The best scientific support for visions of the future has come from developments in quantum physics. In the strange world of the quantum physicist, particles are able to move backward or forward through time, and the same object can be in two or more different places at once.

According to physicist John G. Cramer, future events may send back signals that determine what happens in the present. There is what is called a probability wave from the future as well as one from the past. Where the two probability waves meet, Cramer argues, present reality occurs. Other physicists, such as Fred Alan Wolf, have developed quantum theory into a speculation on "parallel universes." In this extraordinary view of the world, all possible pasts

Professor Roger Penrose
Professor Penrose, a theoretical mathematician at Oxford University, challenged prevailing concepts of past, present, and future in his book The Emperor's New Mind.

FUTURE PARADOX

Someone who foresees a personal disaster may well be able to avoid it — but this invalidates the premonition, which will then never come true.

It is hard to believe that people can foresee the future in dreams or trances unless the future is fixed — in some sense it already exists now or is at least certain to happen. But this poses a problem. If you can foresee the future, surely you can change it. And if you do, the future is not fixed after all.

J. B. Priestley

A nonexistent disaster

There is no paradox involved if a passenger booked on a flight for the following day has a premonitory dream. In his sleep he witnesses an airplane crash in vivid detail and when he wakes up, decides to stay at home. Although it happens without him, the crash occurs just as he dreamed it. He has foreseen the future. But what if it was the pilot of the airliner who had the premonition? He dreams of a crash and so does not take off, instead calling for extra safety checks on the aircraft. As a result, the crash does not happen. But then, what the pilot "foresaw" in his dream was not, as it turned out, the real future. He had a premonition of a disaster that, in fact, never came about.

A famous case of changing the future as the result of a premonitory dream was first reported by Dr. Louise E. Rhine in the *Journal of Parapsychology* (March 1955). According to Dr. Rhine's account, a young woman had dreamed that she was on a camping vacation with her baby son. In her dream, she went down to a nearby river to wash some clothes, taking her child with her. When she arrived at the river, she realized that she had forgotten to bring any soap. Foolishly leaving her child by the riverside, she walked back to the camp. When she returned with the soap, she found that her baby son had fallen into the water and drowned.

Some months later, the mother and child actually did go camping, on a site very similar to the one that had appeared in the dream. The mother went to the river with her baby son to wash some clothes and found that she had forgotten to bring the soap. Suddenly remembering her nightmare, which corresponded to this waking situation in every detail, she picked up her child and took him back to the camp with her to fetch what she needed. Thus possibly — although it cannot be proven — the death of the infant was averted.

Priestley poser

Writers on the paranormal, such as the Russian mystic P. D. Ouspensky and the English researcher J. W. Dunne, have tried to explain this sort of dream in terms of other dimensions of time or alternative "time tracks." In these, possible real futures exist, yet never happen in our time-world. According to this view, the mother's dream was an accurate vision of a future on a parallel track to the one she fortunately chose to take. Discussing this view of the case in his work *Man and Time* (1964), J. B. Priestley put the salient, and so far unanswered, question: "In what world did the baby die?"

P. D. Ouspensky

Time hangs heavy...
The inventor of the time machine makes a tricky connection in the climactic scene of the movie Back to the Future.

BACK TO THE FUTURE
The idea of parallel universes was taken up in the plot of the first of Steven Spielberg's *Back to the Future* series of films, released in 1985. After traveling into the past and interfering with his parents' early relationship, the young hero returns to a world that seems familiar but is radically changed in many ways.

Brave new world
In the new present his father is no longer a failure, a victim of the local bully, and this is reflected in an improvement in the family's material status, the strength of his parents' relationship, and the self-confidence of all their children.

In the fictional world of the movie, the young hero has actually experienced two different versions of the same moment in time.

Parallel universes
This imaginative artist's impression of a series of parallel universes shows clusters of galaxies on the outside of bubblelike spheres. In theory, visions of the future may occur as the bubbles collide in the spacetime continuum.

home run, another in which he strikes out, and so on through every range of possibility. All these futures are sending back probability waves to the present.

Do the twin concepts of probability waves and parallel futures make it possible to foresee the future? Wolf certainly thinks so. In his book *Parallel Universes* (1990), he writes: "If there are

> "If there are parallel futures, all broadcasting back in time to us, surely there are some people who hear them or see them."
> **Fred Alan Wolf**

parallel futures, all broadcasting back in time to us, surely there are some people who hear them or see them....I believe that visionaries are those who are able to turn away from everyday life concerns and tune in to these other worlds, whether they are past-life recalls from parallel worlds gone-by or future-life recalls from worlds yet-to-be."

and futures exist from the beginning of time. At every moment the mind chooses one possibility out of all those available as "reality," but the other parallel universes that have not been chosen still have an existence of a sort.

Probability waves
So this theory suggests that for every pitch in a baseball game there is one universe in which the batter makes it to first base, another in which he hits a

CAN YOU SEE THE FUTURE?

It is a simple matter to test yourself and your friends for clairvoyant abilities.

FOR OVER 50 YEARS researchers into the paranormal have been using a special pack of cards for experiments. These were designed by and are named after an expert in the psychology of perception, Dr. Karl Zener of Duke University.

Zener cards feature five distinct symbols — circle, square, star, cross, and wavy lines. There are 25 cards in a pack, and each symbol appears five times.

There are two simple experiments using Zener cards designed to test for clairvoyance and precognition:

1) Ask a friend to shuffle the cards and then place the top one face down on the table for 30 seconds. At the end of that time, it should be placed face up in a discard pile, and the next card placed face down on the table. Meanwhile, you should be trying to guess each card taken from the pack before it is turned over. You can call out your answer each time so that your friend can record whether it is right or wrong, or you can write it down for checking later.

2) Try to guess, before they are shuffled, the sequence of the 25 cards. Record your impressions, then ask your friend to shuffle the cards, and turn them over, one by one, to check against your answers.

It is important to conduct a number of tests. Normal probability suggests that you will make 5 correct guesses out of 25 each time. This will vary a little on each test. But if you consistently score six or seven, you could well be demonstrating either clairvoyance or precognition in Experiment 1, or precognition in Experiment 2.

Convincing the skeptics

You will need to convince the skeptics that you have eliminated all other possible explanations for the results. Early Zener card tests were criticized because it was felt that hand-shuffling the pack after each trial did not randomize the cards sufficiently. Other critics suggested that in certain lighting it was possible to see the symbol through the back of the card.

To make Experiment 1 as fraud-proof as possible, you and your friend should be in different rooms, with synchronized watches to ensure that the cards are turned over at the agreed intervals. But make sure you record your answer before the end of the 30-second period when the card is revealed. If you don't, your correct answers might be attributed to something else — a successful telepathic exchange with your friend, rather than precognition.

Unmistakable symbols
Zener cards are marked with five different designs. The designs are very simple to avoid any risk of confusion during experiments.

CHAPTER TWO

THE COSMIC CLOCK

A horoscope is a map of the heavens, showing the relative positions of the planets at a particular moment. Astrologers believe that the position of these planets at the time of birth has a bearing on a person's nature and future career.

Humankind has always looked up at the heavens and wondered at the structure and meaning of the stars. As recently as 500 years ago they were thought to form pictures charted upon a great globe — the celestial sphere — that encircled the earth. Some thought that they were tiny holes in the fabric of this sphere, through which traces of a divine light could be seen shining.

Yet within the sphere, and at an unknown distance from earth, there were

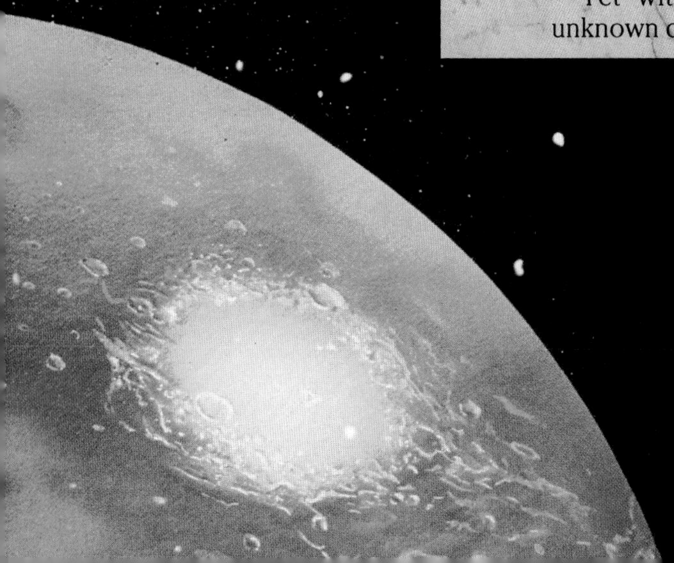

The god Marduk
This dragon is a symbol of the Babylonian god Marduk. Identified with the planet Jupiter, he was deemed to be the chief of the gods. This representation is from the 6th century B.C. and was found on the Ishtar Gate at the ancient site of Babylon, in what is now Iraq.

a few "stars" — and two larger bodies, sun and moon — that seemed to wander at their own pace through the heavens. The Greeks called them "planets," which means "wanderers." Some of these bodies seemed highly capricious in their movements, doubling back on their tracks for days or weeks at a time, while others, particularly the sun and moon, appeared steadily to pursue a predetermined path.

Perhaps even the most primitive people might have identified these wanderers as the gods who influenced lives and events on earth, but the earliest written record comes from the Babylonians. They associated the sun with the god Shamash, bringer of truth and righteousness. At the winter solstice, he rose on the eastern horizon with a group of stars that resembled a horned creature, which the Babylonians named the *kusarikku*, or fish-ram.

The circle of animals
From the house of this fish-ram, which we now call Capricorn, Shamash moved month by month through each of the 12 houses of the zodiac, until he came again to the dark time of the year, and so began his journey again. So the sun's annual passage through the sky was charted by a girdle of star pictures that seemed to turn about the earth. And as most of these pictures were of animals, the Greeks later came to call them the zodiac, which means "circle of animals."

The other wanderers of the heavens included Sin, the moon. Sin moved

THE BABYLONIAN ZODIAC
Over 2,500 years ago, the Babylonians recorded their names for the signs of the zodiac. Most of the modern names for the zodiacal signs that we know today are derived from these characterizations.

Babylonian name	Meaning	Modern name
kusarikku	fish-ram	Capricorn
Enkidu	the giant water-carrier	Aquarius
zibbati	tails	Pisces
hunga	hireling	Aries
gudanna	bull of heaven	Taurus
mastabbagalgal	great twins	Gemini
allul	crab	Cancer
urgula	lion	Leo
absin	furrow	Virgo
zibanitu	scales	Libra
girtab	scorpion	Scorpio
Ninurta	the god of war	Sagittarius

Roman zodiac
This Roman sculpture of the 1st century A.D. depicts the 12 signs of the zodiac. The Roman zodiac is the same as the modern one, and a direct descendant of the Babylonian system.

A LITTLE ASTRONOMY

We can observe the passage of time by the movements of the sun, moon, and planets, carefully charted by astronomers and astrologers over thousands of years.

FOUR THOUSAND YEARS AGO the Babylonian astrologers had a relatively sophisticated understanding of the heavens. They were aware that the stars seemed to revolve once every day above the earth. The sun, moon, and planets also seemed to spin above the earth, although at various speeds.

When the sun rose at dawn, the astrologers could not see which sign of the zodiac was behind it. But if the constellation of Libra rose over the eastern horizon in the evening, the sun at that date had to be "in" Aries, which was on the opposite side of the zodiac circle.

The 12 constellations of the zodiac do not, in fact, occupy equal twelfths of the sky, but for convenience, and to relate them more closely to the months of the year, the circle of the zodiac is divided into 12 equal parts. These are named after the constellations that used to appear in them.

Start of the astrological year

On or about 21 March, the Babylonians observed that the sun "entered" Aries. This was the spring equinox, when night and day are each 12 hours long. From this starting point, the sun entered a new sign every month, until a year later it again entered Aries. The moon moved much faster than the sun, and appeared to enter a new sign every two or three days. Venus and Mercury appeared to keep pace with the Sun, while the other planets moved more slowly, occupying the same sign for months or even years at a time.

But that was 4,000 years ago, and some things have changed. The earth's axis is very slowly wobbling around in a small circle — rather like a top as it begins to slow down. As a result, over the course of 2,000 years, the visible position of the sun at the spring equinox moved through the sign of Aries from 30 degrees to 0 degrees, and at the beginning of the Christian Era it entered Pisces. This phenomenon is called the "precession of the equinoxes."

The age of Aquarius

Now, after nearly another 2,000 years, the sun during the spring equinox is about to enter Aquarius; this is what is meant by "the dawning of the age of Aquarius." But all astrologers, astronomers, and navigators still refer to the spring equinox as 0 degrees of Aries.

A horoscope is a simplified map showing the positions of the planets relative to the earth. The outer circle of the map represents a section through the

Pioneer astronomers
This engraving from Andreas Cellerius's 17th-century atlas Coelestis seu Harmonica Macrocosmica *shows Arab astronomers observing the skies.*

broad band of the zodiac against which the planets appear to move. The earth is at the center of this map. The longitude of the place where a person is born is necessary to draw up that person's horoscope because it allows us to orientate the zodiacal band by working out which sign was overhead at the time of birth, and to calculate the exact positions of the planets.

Leap years

However, the earth does not take exactly 24 hours to revolve on its axis — in fact, it takes 23 hours, 56 minutes, 4.09 seconds — so it has not quite completed its orbit around the sun in 365 days. This is why an extra day must be added to the year every four years, in a leap year — although a day is a little too much, so there is no leap year at the beginning of each century, unless the date is exactly divisible by 400.

Astronomers, who want to point their telescopes at exact positions in the sky, therefore calculate in terms of star time, which they call "sidereal time," based on the precise amount of time the stars take to appear to revolve once about the earth. Astrologers too convert terrestrial time to sidereal time in order to work out the actual positions of the planets at a particular moment.

faster than the sun, passing through all the houses of the zodiac in about 28 days. There were two small, bright planets, Ishtar and Nabu, which we now know as Venus and Mercury. Before the invention of the telescope only three more planets were known, and they were ranked according to brightness and the length of time they took to pass through the zodiac.

The planet Marduk shone steadily with a golden light. This was the god who was known to the Greeks as Zeus, and to the Romans as Jove or Jupiter.

The planet that burned a baleful blood-red in the night was Nergal, god of plagues and war; Ares to the Greeks, and Mars to the Romans. And the slowest mover of all, almost gray in color, was Ningursu, the measurer of time — called Kronos by the Greeks, and Saturn by the Romans.

As they went about the sky on their excursions, sometimes retiring to their own houses, sometimes gathering together as if to confer, the gods seemed to be plotting future events on earth and, possibly, the fate of humanity.

Observing how the movements in the heavens were reflected in events on earth, the priests of Babylon gradually learned how to predict natural phenomena. They kept count of the seasons and could forecast the harvest; they could foretell when the moon would be bright enough to move an

> Observing how the movements in the heavens were reflected in events on earth, the priests of Babylon gradually learned how to predict natural phenomena.

army by night, or dark enough to hide it from its enemies; and they knew the times of future eclipses. And so astrology was born. For centuries the astrologers recorded the movements of the planets and the stars, and about 700 B.C. these were inscribed on thousands of clay tablets for the great library of the Assyrian king Ashurbanipal.

From Assyria, astrology began to spread across the western world. The Egyptians attributed the study of human fate, as it was reflected in the heavens, to Thoth, their god of wisdom, science, and magic. To the Greeks, Thoth was Hermes Trismegistos, "thrice-great Hermes"; the essence of his wisdom was expressed in the principle "as above, so below."

Concentric spheres
Although the Babylonians had visualized the "bowl of night" turning above the earth, it is to the Greeks that we owe the realization that the earth is itself a sphere. They saw the cosmos as successive concentric spheres, turning about the earth as center: each globe was crystal clear and carried one of the seven planets. Beyond the planets spun the starry celestial sphere.

In 280 B.C. the Babylonian Berosus set up a school of astrology on the island of Kos. There all the strands of astrological knowledge from Babylon, Egypt, and Greece became a single thread, and this was disseminated throughout the western world.

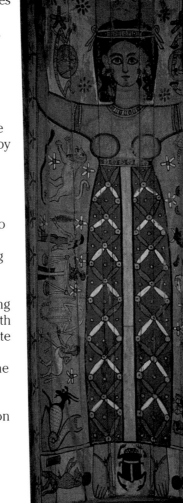

Egyptian zodiac
This sarcophagus interior from the 2nd century A.D. shows the goddess Nut with the 12 signs of the zodiac.

SUN SIGNS

All that most people know of astrology is their sun sign — yet this may convey basic information about their personality.

*E*VERY DAY, ALL OVER THE WORLD, people read their "horoscopes" in newspapers. All those "born under the sign of Aries," they learn, "should be careful in money matters." But these are not real horoscopes, and there is no special significance in "sun signs." If you are Libran, for example, it merely means that you were born when the sun was in Libra – that is, between late September and late October – and it is impossible that everybody with a birthday in those 30 days will suffer the same pains or pleasures.

Nevertheless, the time of year at which an individual is born is thought to have an effect upon personality and physical development. And since the data on which astrological lore is based has been gathered over thousands of years, there might be some truth in the traditional interpretations. But astrologers believe that the positions of the other planets, and which signs are ascendant and descendant, have just as great a bearing on destiny and temperament.

Sun in Aries: Such people are likely to be full of ambition but lacking the patience to carry out long-term schemes. If they feel that they are not properly appreciated they may descend to exasperated, unreasonable behavior, or even deceit.

Sun in Taurus: Taureans are solid and practical. Slow to anger, they may become violent when roused, but they are faithful and generous friends.

Sun in Gemini: Happy, charming, and restless, Geminis are naturally two-faced: they may try hard to be straightforward, but self-interest will at times make them unscrupulous. They seldom lose self-control.

Sun in Cancer: Obstinate, tenacious, and loyal, Cancerians at the same time love the excitement of the crowd. They have excellent memories and are good mimics; they should choose their friends with care.

Sun in Leo: Proud and ambitious, yet sincere and generous, Leos are born leaders. They can go straight to the heart of a problem and carry out long-term plans. But they have a tendency toward boastfulness and narrow-minded conservatism.

Sun in Virgo: Virgos are above all else analytical in temperament. As a result they may prefer to hide their kinder feelings for fear that others may think them to be sentimental.

Sun in Libra: Librans are lovers of comfort and beauty. They have above-average ability to compare things and reach an impartial conclusion, but the urge to criticize must be kept under control.

Sun in Scorpio: Shrewd and self-confident, determined but cautious, Scorpios can offend by their forth-right speech. They can easily make lifelong enemies, but they also make excellent friends.

Sun in Sagittarius: Honesty and truth are important to Sagittarians; they are optimistic, loyal, and very enterprising. They are natural teachers, but may find themselves becoming slaves to convention.

Sun in Capricorn: "Capricious" is a word derived from this sign, and although Capricorns are practical and shrewd, and determined to get to the top, they may suddenly spoil everything with an outbreak of irresponsibility.

Sun in Aquarius: Quiet and refined, Aquarians are also strong and forceful, capable of great resistance to fatigue. At times they reveal unreasonable anger, at other times they are the "life and soul of the party."

Sun in Pisces: Pisceans are sympathetic and tactful, and willing to listen and learn. They may be oversensitive, but are generally friendly and easygoing. However, they sometimes tend to lack concentration, and may find it difficult to plan their careers.

Zodiacal man
This 14th-century zodiac is from the French duke de Berry's Book of Hours.

Anybody can draw up a horoscope; in the following pages we show you how to do it.

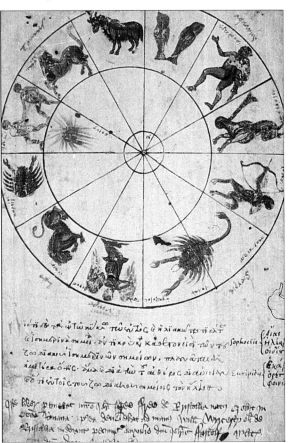

A HOROSCOPE IS a stylized map of the heavens, showing the positions of the planets, including the sun and the moon, against the background of the circle of the zodiac, at the moment of a person's birth. You do not need esoteric knowledge to cast a horoscope: it is not too difficult to draw one up using astronomers' tables or a nautical almanac. If you want to develop a fuller understanding of the subject you can buy a book called an ephemeris, which sets out tables of planetary positions that are listed month by month and year by year. An ephemeris is available at any good bookstore.

Making a start

The first step in drawing up the horoscope is to correct the local time (LT) of the subject's birth into Greenwich Mean Time (GMT). To do this, you must establish which time zone the subject was born in and add or subtract the time difference from GMT. It is important to remember that some countries adjust their clocks by an hour in the summer in order to make the most of daylight. This is known as Daylight Saving Time and must be allowed for in calculating GMT.

Celestial orbit

Once you have established the correct GMT for the birth of your subject, the next step is to convert the GMT into sidereal time, or star time (ST). Sidereal time represents the time it takes for the celestial sphere to revolve around the earth.

It is necessary to establish the correct stage of this cycle, so that the accurate positions of the planets at the time of birth can be calculated. It is generally accepted that the earth revolves on its axis once every 24 hours. However, this revolution actually takes only 23 hours 56 minutes and 4.09 seconds. You therefore need to make certain adjustments in order to obtain an accurate ST. This is done by some simple arithmetical calculations (see table at left).

The figures shown in the table apply only for the longitude of Greenwich, England, which is 0 degrees. A further adjustment needs to be made for different

Medieval zodiac
This drawing is from a late 14th-century astronomical treatise, written in Greek, from Constantinople (now Istanbul, Turkey). It looks like a modern zodiac except that Scorpio appears to take up two divisions, and Libra seems to be missing. This is because in Greek astronomy the sign of Libra was sometimes called "the Claws or Balance." The sign of Libra is therefore represented by the claws of the Scorpion.

SIDEREAL TIME
This table shows ST at midnight on December 31/January 1

31

1904–23:

1904 and all leap years:	06:37
The following year:	06:40
Next year:	06:39
Next year:	06:38
This pattern repeats until 1924:	
1924 (and all leap years):	06:38
1925:	06:41
1926:	06:40
1927:	06:39
1928 (leap year):	06:38
This pattern repeats until 1956:	
1956 (and all leap years):	06:39
1957:	06:42
1958:	06:41
1959:	06:40
This pattern repeats until 1986:	
1986:	06:41
1987:	06:39
1988 (and all leap years):	06:40
1989:	06:43

Continue reducing by 1 min. per year but add 3 mins. in the year after a leap year. To find the ST at any time in the year, use the next set of tables:

ADD FOR THE MONTH

| | Common year | | Leap year |

JAN	FEB	MAR	APR
h m	h m	h m	h m
0 0	2 2	3 52	5 55
0 0	2 2	3 56	5 59

MAY	JUNE	JULY	AUG
h m	h m	h m	h m
7 53	9 55	11 54	13 56
7 57	9 59	11 58	14 00

SEPT	OCT	NOV	DEC
h m	h m	h m	h m
15 58	17 56	19 59	21 57
16 02	18 00	20 02	22 01

ADD FOR THE DAY

1st: 0m **2nd:** 4m **3rd:** 8m **4th:** 12m **5th:** 16m **6th:** 20m **7th:** 24m **8th:** 28m **9th:** 32m **10th:** 35m **11th:** 39m **12th:** 43m **13th:** 47m **14th:** 51m **15th:** 55m **16th:** 59m **17th:** 1h 3m **18th:** 1h 7m **19th:** 1h 11m **20th:** 1h 15m **21st:** 1h 19m **22nd:** 1h 23m **23rd:** 1h 27m **24th:** 1h 31m **25th:** 1h 35m **26th:** 1h 39m **27th:** 1h 42m **28th:** 1h 46m **29th:** 1h 50m **30th:** 1h 54m **31st:** 1h 58m

ADD FOR THE HOURS

1	2	3	4	5	6	7	8	9	10	11	12
0	0	1	1	1	1	1	1	1	2	2	2

(minutes)

Heart of the universe
This 17th-century engraving from Andreas Cellerius's atlas Coelestis seu Harmonica Macrocosmica *(1660) illustrates the Ptolemaic view of the universe. The earth is depicted at the center of the universe and the sun, planets, and the stars are shown revolving around the earth.*

longitudes. This can be simplified and calculated thus: for each degree of longitude west, subtract 4 minutes from the ST you have calculated; for each degree of longitude east, add 4 minutes to the ST. For example, to work out the ST for a person who was born in New York City, the following adjustment is

You do not need esoteric knowledge to cast a horoscope.

made: New York is located on longitude 74 degrees west, so this means that 74 x 4 minutes (4 h 56 m) must be subtracted from the ST to give an accurate reading.

A worked example

To show you how to draw up a horoscope we have taken as an example a person who was born at 6:22 P.M. (that is, 1822 on the 24-hour clock)

on April 20, 1889, on the Austro-German border, at longitude 13 degrees east. Although a European standard time was not adopted in Austria or Germany until 1891, it is fairly certain that the local time of 1822 hours converts to 1722 GMT.

CALCULATION TO FIND SIDEREAL TIME		
The ST at midnight		
on January 1, 1889, was:	*06 h*	*43 m*
Addition for month		
(see ST table):	*05 h*	*55 m*
Addition for day:	*01 h*	*15 m*
Addition for the hours		
(17 hours 22 minutes):		*3 m*
GMT:	*17 h*	*22 m*
Addition for longitude, 13 x 4:		*52 m*
Total	**32h**	**10 m**

Since the ST represents one revolution of the celestial sphere every 24 hours, we can subtract 24 hours from this total and calculate the ST as 8 hours 10 minutes in this particular birth chart.

ASTROLOGICAL TABLES

These simplified tables will enable you to work out the positions of the midheaven, the moon, and the sun when you are drawing up your horoscope.

Position of the midheaven

Just as time on a clock is told from the top (representing 0, 12, or 24 hours), so sidereal time (ST) is measured from the moment when 0 degrees Aries is in the midheaven or *medium coeli* (MC). The MC moves about 1 degree every 4 minutes. Calculate the position within the hour from the following figures.

ST	MC	ST	MC
00.00	0 degrees Aries	13.00	16 degrees Libra
01.00	16 degrees Aries	14.00	2 degrees Scorpio
02.00	2 degrees Taurus	15.00	17 degrees Scorpio
03.00	17 degrees Taurus	16.00	2 degrees Sagittarius
04.00	2 degrees Gemini	17.00	16 degrees Sagittarius
05.00	16 degrees Gemini	18.00	0 degrees Capricorn
06.00	0 degrees Cancer	19.00	14 degrees Capricorn
07.00	14 degrees Cancer	20.00	28 degrees Capricorn
08.00	28 degrees Cancer	21.00	13 degrees Aquarius
09.00	13 degrees Leo	22.00	28 degrees Aquarius
10.00	28 degrees Leo	23.00	14 degrees Pisces
11.00	14 degrees Virgo	24.00	0 degrees Aries
12.00	0 degrees Libra		

Position of the sun

This table shows the position of the sun at midnight GMT on the first of the month. (These figures are approximate, and vary — but not significantly — from year to year.) The sun moves about 1 degree a day.

JAN:	10 degrees Capricorn	JUL:	10 degrees Cancer
FEB:	12 degrees Aquarius	AUG:	9 degrees Leo
MAR:	11 degrees Pisces	SEP:	9 degrees Virgo
APR:	12 degrees Aries	OCT:	8 degrees Libra
MAY:	11 degrees Taurus	NOV:	9 degrees Scorpio
JUN:	11 degrees Gemini	DEC:	9 degrees Sagittarius

Position of the moon

The moon moves much faster than any other planet — some 13 degrees per day. The following table gives the position of the moon for midnight, GMT, on January 1.

To estimate the approximate position of the moon, add on about 13 degrees for each day, remembering that the sign changes every 30 degrees, and that 360 degrees make a complete zodiac circle. For hours during the day, add 1 degree for every two hours, plus one extra degree for any time after midday.

1921	8 degrees Libra	1961	29 degrees Gemini
1922	11 degrees Aquarius	1962	0 degrees Scorpio
1923	14 degrees Gemini	1963	13 degrees Pisces
1924	25 degrees Libra	1964	1 degree Leo
1925	29 degrees Pisces	1965	19 degrees Sagittarius
1926	1 degree Leo	1966	19 degrees Aries
1927	4 degrees Sagittarius	1967	6 degrees Virgo
1928	17 degrees Aries	1968	22 degrees Capricorn
1929	20 degrees Virgo	1969	9 degrees Gemini
1930	21 degrees Capricorn	1970	10 degrees Libra
1931	24 degrees Taurus	1971	28 degrees Aquarius
1932	10 degrees Libra	1972	12 degrees Cancer
1933	10 degrees Pisces	1973	1 degree Sagittarius
1934	11 degrees Cancer	1974	1 degree Aries
1935	16 degrees Scorpio	1975	19 degrees Leo
1936	2 degrees Taurus	1976	2 degrees Capricorn
1937	0 degrees Virgo	1977	20 degrees Taurus
1938	1 degree Capricorn	1978	22 degrees Virgo
1939	5 degrees Taurus	1979	11 degrees Aquarius
1940	26 degrees Virgo	1980	23 degrees Gemini
1941	19 degrees Aquarius	1981	9 degrees Scorpio
1942	22 degrees Gemini	1982	13 degrees Pisces
1943	25 degrees Libra	1983	2 degrees Leo
1944	18 degrees Pisces	1984	13 degrees Sagittarius
1945	9 degrees Leo	1985	29 degrees Aries
1946	12 degrees Sagittarius	1986	5 degrees Virgo
1947	16 degrees Taurus	1987	23 degrees Capricorn
1948	9 degrees Virgo	1988	4 degrees Gemini
1949	29 degrees Capricorn	1989	18 degrees Libra
1950	1 degree Gemini	1990	26 degrees Aquarius
1951	7 degrees Libra	1991	14 degrees Cancer
1952	29 degrees Aquarius	1992	25 degrees Scorpio
1953	18 degrees Cancer	1993	8 degrees Aries
1954	20 degrees Virgo	1994	18 degrees Leo
1955	29 degrees Pisces	1995	4 degrees Capricorn
1956	20 degrees Leo	1996	16 degrees Taurus
1957	8 degrees Capricorn	1997	28 degrees Virgo
1958	11 degrees Taurus	1998	10 degrees Aquarius
1959	21 degrees Virgo	1999	25 degrees Gemini
1960	10 degrees Aquarius	2000	6 degrees Scorpio

Calculating the midheaven

Before we can begin to mark the planets on the birth chart we must establish what sign of the zodiac is in the overhead position at the moment of birth. This is called the midheaven, or *medium coeli* (MC) by astrologers.

If you look at the table at left, for the position of the midheaven you will see that at ST 8:00 the MC is at 28 degrees Cancer. Since the MC moves 1 degree every 4 minutes, at 8:10 it will be at 28

> **Both the ascendant and the descendant signs will have great significance when it comes to interpreting the birth chart.**

Cancer + 2.5 degrees = 0.5 degrees Leo. For practical purposes, we can call this 1 degree Leo. Having established that Leo is in the overhead position, it is now possible to orient the circle of the horoscope. This resembles a compass rose that is turned upside down: therefore, south is at the top, north at the bottom, and east and west to left and right respectively. Because of the direction in which the earth rotates, the zodiac appears to rise sign by sign over

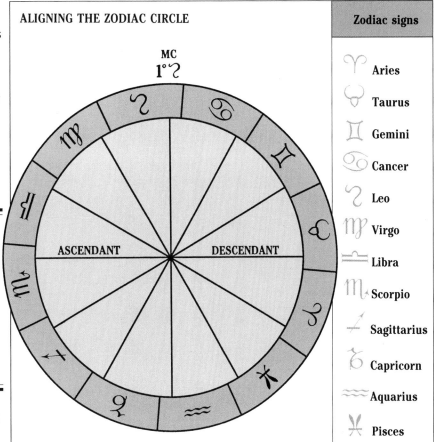

ALIGNING THE ZODIAC CIRCLE

MC
1° ♌

ASCENDANT   DESCENDANT

Zodiac signs

♈ Aries
♉ Taurus
♊ Gemini
♋ Cancer
♌ Leo
♍ Virgo
♎ Libra
♏ Scorpio
♐ Sagittarius
♑ Capricorn
♒ Aquarius
♓ Pisces

the eastern horizon, and the signs are therefore inserted in the chart in a counterclockwise sequence.

Rising and falling signs

In our example the MC is marked in due south (at the top of the chart) at 1 degree Leo, and the 12 houses in equal twelfths around the chart. The sign rising over the eastern horizon (which falls on the left side of the chart) at the moment of birth is Scorpio, which is called the ascendant. The sign that falls on the opposite side of the chart to the ascendant is called the descendant which in this birth chart is Taurus. Both the ascendant and the descendant signs will have great significance when it comes to interpreting the birth chart.

Moon changes

Once the MC has been found and the zodiac circle correctly aligned, the next step is to calculate the position of the moon. The table at left shows how to do this. In this example, at midnight on January 1, 1889, the position of the moon was 29 degrees Sagittarius. On January 1, 1890, it was at 12 degrees Taurus. This

Starting your horoscope
Before drawing up a horoscope, it is important to be sure that you recognize each of the 12 symbols of the zodiac (shown above). In this chart we demonstrate the first steps in drawing up your horoscope. The MC is marked — at 1 degree Leo — after which the alignment of the signs of the zodiac can be made. Next, the eastern and western horizons are marked in, pinpointing the ascendant sign, Scorpio, and the descendant sign, Taurus.

Fixing the future
This 16th-century English woodcut shows an astrologer recording the moment of birth. The exact time is vital to the accuracy of the horoscope.

Uranus

Neptune

THE NEW PLANETS

Three of the planets in our solar system were discovered only relatively recently. The planet Uranus was spotted in 1781, Neptune in 1846, and Pluto in 1930. There is therefore no traditional body of knowledge concerning the astrological significance of these three planets, and astrologers have argued among themselves whether they should be included in the horoscope.

Slow-moving planets

Because they are so far away, all three planets seem to move very slowly, occupying the same part of the zodiac for months or years at a time, and they therefore appear in the same position in the horoscopes of people born at widely differing dates.

However, their appearance in the 12 houses of the horoscope changes throughout every 24 hours, and their position relative to other planets varies, as these others move more rapidly.

Modern astrologers have developed an explanation of the significance of these planets in areas not covered by traditional astrology: magic, mysticism, and other spiritual matters.

represents the total number of degrees the moon has passed through during the year. It always makes 13 complete circuits of the earth, so the number of degrees it has passed through is 13 x 360 = 4680 plus an incomplete circuit. The incomplete circuit includes four more signs (4 x 30 = 120 degrees), plus 13 odd degrees. This gives a total of 4813 degrees. Divided by 365, this gives a total of 13.19 degrees per day.

It is difficult to determine the exact moment of birth, so the moon's precise position in a natal horoscope is often doubtful.

By April 20, 109 days had passed: 109 x 13.19 = 1438 degrees, just 3 degrees less than four complete circuits of 360 degrees. The moon is therefore at 27 degrees Sagittarius. By 6:00 P.M., the moon will have advanced a further 10 degrees, to 7 degrees Capricorn.

It is important to remember that this is only an approximate method of calculating the position of the moon. In

certain months the moon seems to move more slowly, due to the angle of its orbit with the equator. However, if you do not have access to a detailed ephemeris, this method can be used. It is difficult to determine the exact moment of birth, so the moon's precise position in a natal horoscope is often doubtful.

Next to be marked is the sun. The sun moves only 29 degrees during the 30 days of April, so that on April 20 it will have moved 18 degrees forward from 12 degrees Aries. This puts the sun on the cusp, that is, between Aries and Taurus (30 degrees Aries being the same as 0 degrees Taurus).

Planetary places

An ephemeris is necessary to find the positions of the other planets. Because of the apparently erratic movement of some, there is no space to tabulate them here. Mercury and Venus are always near the Sun, and the ephemeris gives their positions as:

Mercury: *25 degrees Aries*
Venus: *16 degrees Taurus*

Because the path of the planet Venus is viewed from Earth against the background of the stars, it appears to be moving backward through Taurus at this time, from 19 degrees Taurus on April 10 to 3 degrees Taurus on May 22. Venus is said to be "retrograde" (backward-moving) during this period.

The ephemeris shows the positions of the other planets as follows:

Mars: *17 degrees Taurus*
Jupiter: *8 degrees Capricorn*
Saturn: *13 degrees Leo*
Uranus: *19 degrees Libra, retrograde*
Neptune: *1 degree Gemini*
Pluto: *4 degrees Gemini*

All the planets can now be marked on the chart, ready for interpretation.

Astrological aspects

The sun is close to setting on the western horizon, while the moon will not rise for several hours. What astrologers find of particular significance

ZODIACAL INFLUENCES

Most people know their sun sign: whether they are Leo or Cancer. But the position of the moon, and the zodiacal sign ascending over the eastern horizon at the time of birth may be of greater significance.

MOON

The sign of the zodiac in which the moon appeared when you were born is believed by astrologers to indicate what type of temperament and outlook you will have on life.

Moon in Aries: Indicates emotional instability, but also great independence, and a temper that is seldom lost for long.
Moon in Taurus: Emotional stability and a need for physical security predominate. Encouragement may be needed to start an enterprise, but it will be carried through with persistence.
Moon in Gemini: Nervous, restless temperament, which may show itself in ceaseless fidgeting and chatter; but resourceful and with a quick imagination.
Moon in Cancer: Deeply emotional, with a love of home life. An awareness of the feelings of others that is almost telepathic.
Moon in Leo: Inclined to self-dramatization, with a need to be admired and loved. Insistence on cleanliness and good behavior.
Moon in Virgo: Shy personality, and an obsession with detail. Diet and health of constant concern.
Moon in Libra: Charming but easily swayed by others' advice, which may lead to accepting ideas that are not well thought out.
Moon in Scorpio: Stubborn adherence to selfish ideas; personal affairs taken seriously, with a tendency to jealousy and revenge.
Moon in Sagittarius: Idealistic nature; dedication to conventional religion or philosophy, with a danger of bigotry.
Moon in Capricorn: Cold and cautious disposition; ambitious.
Moon in Aquarius: Kindly, but never deeply involved emotionally.
Moon in Pisces: Deeply affected by the thoughts and emotions of others, and therefore very easily hurt.

ASCENDANTS

Astrologers believe that the sign of the zodiac ascending in the east at the moment of birth determines your physical appearance, as well as any health problems you may encounter.

Ascendant in Aries: Average stature, lean and long body; broad head with narrower chin. Prone to nervous disorders and kidney trouble.
Ascendant in Taurus: Average to short stature, with a heavy, thickset body; broad forehead. A tendency to respiratory ailments.
Ascendant in Gemini: Tall, thin, upright body, long face; active movements, and very expressive hands. Weak constitution.
Ascendant in Cancer: Average to short stature; fleshy body and short legs; a round face, with prominent forehead. Prone to gastric disorders.
Ascendant in Leo: Stature above average, with big-boned and well-built body; a stately carriage. Subject to heart disease and back pains.
Ascendant in Virgo: Well-knit, even plump, body of above average stature; oval face. Worry about diet affects the gastric system.
Ascendant in Libra: Average stature; round face. Health at risk from excessive eating and drinking.
Ascendant in Scorpio: Strong thick body of average stature, generally rather hairy; square face. Generally strong but tendency to ailments of bladder or genitals.
Ascendant in Sagittarius: Above-average height; oval face; expressive eyes; a tendency to baldness. Highly strung; hips and thighs susceptible to disease.
Ascendant in Capricorn: Below average height; bony body; long and angular face. Constitution strong, but tendency to depression, skin disorders, and possibly leg trouble.
Ascendant in Aquarius: Below average stature; thick-set; good complexion. Weak constitution.
Ascendant in Pisces: Slightly below average stature, with fleshy body and short, thick limbs; largish face with pale complexion. Tendency to boils and ulcers.

Moonstruck
Italian writer Alighieri Dante created a vision of heaven and hell in The Divine Comedy *(c.1510) in which the planets exerted a powerful influence. This 16th-century painting shows the heroine Beatrice traveling with Dante to the moon.*

PLANETARY HOUSES

The horoscope is divided into 12 equal houses. They are numbered counterclockwise, starting from the ascendant, which always falls in the first house.

Governing influences

Each house governs some aspect of the individual's destiny.

House 1: The appearance and personality of the individual.

House 2: Money and portable possessions, income, and finances.

House 3: Intelligence, communications, close relationships.

House 4: The home and mother.

House 5: Procreation, love, children, and sexual compatibility; possibly also pleasures, gambling.

House 6: Servants, employment, illness and recovery.

House 7: Marriage and other partnerships.

House 8: Death and inheritance.

House 9: Travel and exploration (both geographical and spiritual), the law, and the church.

House 10: Fame, notoriety, career; and also the father.

House 11: Social position, friends, societies and organizations.

House 12: Secrecy, concealment, the subconscious, psychic faculties; and also unknown enemies.

is the positions of the planets relative to one another. These are known as the aspects of the planets.

The Moon and Jupiter are very close together; when this occurs the planets are said to be in conjunction (within not more than 8 degrees of each other). On this chart Venus and Mars are also in conjunction. The effect of conjunction is to enhance the influences that are associated with each planet — just as a conjunction of sun and moon produces floodtides on earth. Planets are termed in opposition when they are separated by approximately 180 degrees. Planets that are about 90 degrees apart form what is called a square. A trine is formed when the planets are about 120 degrees apart.

The interpretation

In this birth chart the Moon and Jupiter are in conjunction, and they are in trine with the Sun. This is a good aspect. But the Moon and Jupiter are also nearly square — which is a bad aspect — to Uranus and Mercury. The Sun is in opposition to Uranus, which is another bad aspect.

The ascendant is Scorpio, indicating what this man's physical type could be: a sturdy body of average height; a slightly bullet-shaped head covered with thick, coarse hair; a rather square face but with a sharp nose. This man may have been generally resistant to disease, but he might have suffered from ailments of the bladder and genitals.

An ambitious man

The sun is on the cusp between Aries and Taurus. Those with sun on the cusp tend to show the bad characteristics of both signs, and this man would have been full of ambition and almost impossible to divert from his purpose; any opposition to him is apt to have engendered fits of uncontrollable rage.

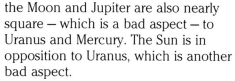

Planet Signs

☉ Sun
☽ Moon
☿ Mercury
♀ Venus
♂ Mars
♃ Jupiter
♄ Saturn
♅ Uranus
♆ Neptune
♇ Pluto

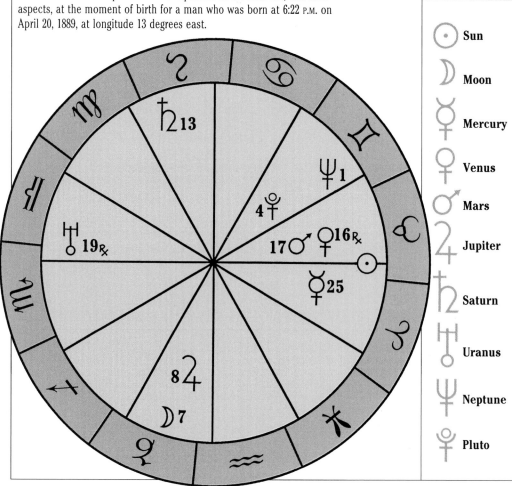

THE COMPLETED NATAL HOROSCOPE
This chart shows the positions of the planets in the heavens, and their aspects, at the moment of birth for a man who was born at 6:22 P.M. on April 20, 1889, at longitude 13 degrees east.

Warlike planet
The planet Mars has always been associated with a military-minded or aggressive personality. Its position in this birth chart indicates fierce ambition.

Such a person might well have harbored resentment for a long time until he could find a suitable opportunity for exacting his revenge.

Positive characteristics

The more positive characteristics of this person's birth chart would have been the enthusiasm with which he entered into new projects and the way in which he could communicate with others. Persuasive in argument, he was probably given to exaggeration.

The moon in Capricorn signifies a cold, emotionally cautious character. The ambition denoted by the sun's position is reinforced, and this man is likely to have been selfish and materialistic.

Mercury in Aries suggests a person who is quick-thinking and fond of argument. However, this man would be likely to have been persuaded by the force of his own proposals, driving ahead to implement them without giving proper consideration to the outcome.

Venus and Mars conjunct in Taurus, with Venus retrograde, are in the seventh house, traditionally associated with partnerships, such as marriage. This could suggest that this person tried to be dominant in his sexual relationships, but that he was a poor lover, either physically or emotionally.

The final analysis

Jupiter in Capricorn indicates a conservative approach to matters of social change, and a dogged insistence upon traditional family values. Saturn is retrograde in Leo, and so represents the worst of everything that Leo stands for: a lust for power, bigotry, egotism, and a desire for imposing discipline. Combined with Jupiter in Capricorn and Uranus retrograde in Libra, it indicates a man determined to impose his conservative beliefs on others.

A violent death

Neptune, representing spiritual feelings, is on the cusp of Taurus and Gemini, and shows little influence in the horoscope. But Pluto, brooding in the eighth house, associated with death, forebodes a sudden and violent end.

There are other things to be read in this horoscope, but most serve only to emphasize the indications already outlined. You will probably not be surprised to learn that this is the birth chart of Adolf Hitler.

> Pluto, brooding in the eighth house, associated with death, forebodes a violent and sudden end.

CHINESE HOROSCOPES

Chinese astrology, based on the phases of the moon, is mainly concerned with an individual's character and his or her relations with others.

Rat
1912 (water), 1924 (wood),
1936 (fire), 1948 (earth),
1960 (metal), 1972 (water),
1984 (wood), 1996 (fire)

Buffalo
1913 (water), 1925 (wood),
1937 (fire), 1949 (earth),
1961 (metal), 1973 (water),
1985 (wood), 1997 (fire)

Tiger
1914 (wood), 1926 (fire),
1938 (earth), 1950 (metal),
1962 (water), 1974 (wood),
1986 (fire), 1998 (earth)

Cat
1915 (wood), 1927 (fire),
1939 (earth), 1951 (metal),
1963 (water), 1975 (wood),
1987 (fire), 1999 (earth)

Dragon
1916 (fire), 1928 (earth),
1940 (metal), 1952 (water),
1964 (wood), 1976 (fire),
1988 (earth), 2000 (metal)

Snake
1917 (fire), 1929 (earth),
1941 (metal), 1953 (water),
1965 (wood), 1977 (fire),
1989 (earth), 2001 (metal)

YOUR ANIMAL SIGN

The year you were born in determines your animal sign. There are 12 signs, and they change each year, at the Chinese New Year. On this and the facing page is a list of the animals and some of their years, with the appropriate movable modifying agents. By working back from these dates you can find out the animal sign and movable agent for any year. The sequence that Chinese horoscopes follow is: Rat, Buffalo, Tiger, Cat, Dragon, Snake, Horse, Goat, Monkey, Rooster, Dog, and Pig.

Movable years

The Chinese New Year can fall anywhere between January 20 and February 20. People born before the New Year date belong to the previous year's sign. See opposite for a list of Chinese New Years.

WESTERN ASTROLOGY LAYS more emphasis on making actual predictions about the future than the Chinese version of the art. Another difference is that Western astrologers place great reliance on the sun and the movements of the planets to form their charts, while the Chinese are mainly concerned with the phases of the moon.

But Western and Eastern horoscopes have some features in common. For example, they both use 12 signs. In Chinese astrology, the signs are all named after animals. Chinese horoscopes were in widespread use more than 3,000 years ago, and the system has evolved over the centuries. In some systems the fourth sign is known as the Cat, but in others as the Rabbit, and the Goat is also known as the Sheep. This is because the Chinese characters denoting these animals are vague in their meaning, and different animals have been attributed to them.

The influence of the moon

The moon is indeed crucial to Chinese horoscopes. More than any other heavenly body, it is reputed to influence behavior on earth. The expression "lunatic," for example, was formerly used about people whose mental disturbances were ascribed to lunar movements. The moon also governs the tides. Since water seems particularly affected by it, and since our bodies are roughly 90 percent liquid, the moon may indeed have a noticeable effect on us.

The characteristics attributed to each animal are complex and sometimes surprisingly precise: the Snake, for instance, is said to adore accessories, and Rats love sweets. However, the following brief descriptions offer an easy introduction to the 12 signs. Rats are born under the sign of charm; Buffaloes under the twin signs of equilibrium and tenacity; Tigers under the sign of courage; Cats under the sign of virtue; Dragons under the sign of luck; Snakes under the sign of wisdom; Horses under the twin signs of elegance and ardor; Goats under the sign of art; Monkeys under the sign of fantasy; Roosters under the sign of candor; Dogs under the sign of loyalty; Pigs under the sign of honesty.

Hour signs

Much as Western signs have ascendants and descendants, Chinese horoscopes have, at first appearance, a frighteningly complicated substructure of attendant signs and modifying agents. Of these the most influential are the hour signs. There are only 12 hours in a traditional Chinese day, each hour lasting two Western hours. These 12 hours are also named after the same animals as the years, and follow the same sequence. The first Chinese hour, between 11:00 P.M. and 1:00 A.M., is the hour of the Rat; the Buffalo is next, between 1:00 A.M. and 3:00 A.M., and so on. The hour sign adds an important dimension to the year sign. The year sign dominates the permanent character, whereas hour signs influence more superficial, day-to-day activities. A Dragon with a Pig hour, for example, will still be impetuous but also over-concerned about his or her appearance.

Another important modifying factor is the role of the five agents. These are water, wood, earth, fire, and metal. Each animal has a fixed agent: the Rat, Buffalo, and Pig have water; the Tiger, Cat, and Dragon have wood; the Snake, Horse, and Goat have fire; and the Monkey, Rooster, and Dog have metal. (Earth is not attributed as a fixed agent, since it is deemed to be found in each of the other four agents.)

Chinese horoscopes have a complicated substructure of attendant signs and modifying agents.

Each animal also has a movable agent, which changes every 10 years, in the following sequence: metal, water, wood, fire, earth. The Dragon, for example, has wood as its fixed agent, and a Dragon born in 1940 has metal as its movable agent. Wood and metal can be used to make an ax; this is therefore deemed to be an auspicious mix. A Dragon born in the year 1952 will still have wood as its fixed agent, but water will be its movable agent.

Marital compatibility
Chinese horoscopes are used throughout China as a means of establishing positive and enduring relationships. In China, before a couple is married, hours are spent going over the various signs, agents, and their modifying factors to discover as many compatible influences as possible. Indeed, if there are not enough, it is likely that the couple will not be allowed to marry.

No matter where the Chinese settle, the 12 animal signs and their modifying factors are used daily as a way of understanding more fully the hand that life has dealt them. Most of the people believe that everyone can learn the truth about themselves and those close to them through astrology, the Chinese continue to place their horoscopes at the very heart of their way of life.

Horse
1918 (earth), 1930 (metal),
1942 (water), 1954 (wood),
1966 (fire), 1978 (earth),
1990 (metal), 2002 (water)

Goat
1919 (earth), 1931 (metal),
1943 (water), 1955 (wood),
1967 (fire), 1979 (earth),
1991 (metal), 2003 (water)

Monkey
1920 (metal), 1932 (water),
1944 (wood), 1956 (fire),
1968 (earth), 1980 (metal),
1992 (water), 2004 (wood)

Rooster
1921 (metal), 1933 (water),
1945 (wood), 1957 (fire),
1969 (earth), 1981 (metal),
1993 (water), 2005 (wood)

Dog
1922 (water), 1934 (wood),
1946 (fire), 1958 (earth),
1970 (metal), 1982 (water),
1994 (wood), 2006 (fire)

Pig
1923 (water), 1935 (wood),
1947 (fire), 1959 (earth),
1971 (metal), 1983 (water),
1995 (wood), 2007 (fire)

CHINESE NEW YEAR DATES FOR THE YEARS 1912–2000:
2/18/12; 2/6/13; 1/26/14; 2/14/15;
2/3/16; 1/23/17; 2/11/18; 2/1/19;
2/20/20; 2/8/21; 1/28/22; 2/16/23;
2/5/24; 1/25/25; 2/13/26; 2/2/27;
1/23/28; 2/10/29; 1/30/30; 2/17/31;
2/6/32; 1/26/33; 2/14/34; 2/4/35;
1/24/36; 2/11/37; 1/31/38; 2/19/39;
2/8/40; 1/27/41; 2/15/42; 2/5/43;
1/25/44; 2/13/45; 2/2/46; 1/22/47;
2/10/48; 1/29/49; 2/17/50; 2/6/51;
1/27/52; 2/14/53; 2/3/54; 1/24/55;
2/12/56; 1/31/57; 2/18/58; 2/8/59;
1/28/60; 2/15/61; 2/5/62; 1/25/63;
2/13/64; 2/12/65; 1/21/66; 2/9/67;
1/30/68; 2/17/69; 2/6/70; 1/27/71;
1/16/72; 2/3/73; 1/23/74; 2/11/75;
1/31/76; 2/18/77; 2/7/78; 1/28/79;
2/16/80; 2/4/81; 1/25/82; 2/13/83;
2/2/84; 2/20/85; 2/9/86; 1/29/87;
2/17/88; 2/6/89; 1/27/90; 2/15/91;
2/4/92; 1/23/93; 2/10/94; 1/31/95;
2/19/96; 2/8/97; 1/28/98 ; 2/6/99;
1/27/2000.

ASTROLOGY AND THE SCIENTISTS

For centuries astronomers and other scientists have heaped scorn on astrology. But recent research has suggested that the planets may indeed be influencing us more than we think.

Sir Isaac Newton
This English physicist and mathematician is famous as the discoverer of gravity. His research into the influence on earth of the other heavenly bodies led him to an interest in astrology.

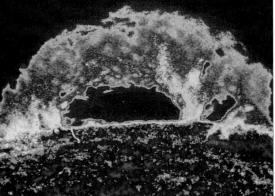

Solar flare
Modern technology enables sunspot activity to be monitored and photographed by scientists attempting to establish its cause. This is a computer-enhanced photograph of a solar explosion.

*I*N THE EARLY 18TH CENTURY the astronomer Edmond Halley, discoverer of the comet that bears his name, quarreled with Sir Isaac Newton at a scientific meeting. Halley mocked Newton for believing in astrology. Newton replied stiffly: "I, sir, have studied the subject; you have not."

It is now known that the relative positions of sun and moon produce the terrestrial tides. There is reason to suppose that the planets — and in particular the huge, heavy planets such as Jupiter, Saturn, Uranus, and Neptune — may produce similar tides in the liquid core of the Sun. It is also accepted that the emission of cosmic rays from the sun is affected by the ebb and flow of its tides. Is it irrational, therefore, to suggest that the level of cosmic radiation at any time — influenced, at least in part, by the planetary positions — might affect a person born at that time?

One of the first pieces of research along these lines was carried out not by an astronomer or astrologer but by an engineer, John Nelson of RCA Communications, Inc. He knew that unusual sunspot activity was followed by serious interruptions of radio communication, and in 1940 he began to collect data in an attempt to predict this effect.

Predicting cosmic storms

By 1967, Nelson could claim a 93 percent success rate in his predictions of forthcoming cosmic storms; this was based on a total of 1,460 forecasts. He had discovered that there was an apparent correlation between intense solar disturbance and the relative positions of the planets — that is, their aspects. Severe magnetic storms occurred when one of the four inner

William Lilly

FIRE FROM HEAVEN?

In 1648 the Englishman William Lilly wrote: "In the year 1665...or near that year...there will appear in this kingdom so strange a revolution of fate, so grand a catastrophe as never yet appeared....It will be ominous to London, to all sorts of people...by reason of sundry fires and a consuming plague."

In 1664 he returned to the subject, publishing a broadsheet illustrated with woodcuts, including one that showed the sign of Gemini (traditionally that of the City of London) plunging into flames.

Bubonic plague

A year later, in 1665, London was visited by a major outbreak of bubonic plague, followed in 1666 by the fire that destroyed much of the city.

Lilly's prediction of the plague received wide publicity, and when the fire broke out in the following year it was suggested in Parliament that he himself had started it in order to enhance his standing as a prophet. He was arrested and, only after a long investigation, cleared of all suspicion — a verdict that made his reputation forever.

planets — Mercury, Venus, Earth, or the Moon — was at an angle of 0, 90, or 180 degrees with another planet farther from the Sun; there were also periods of solar calm when two or more planets were at angles of 60 or 120 degrees apart.

It is an interesting coincidence that Mercury, the planet traditionally associated in astrology with communication, appeared to have the most significant role. As Guy Lyon Playfair and Scott Hill put it in their book *The Cycles of Heaven* (1978): "Nelson's work is an example of what astrology may once have been and still could be: the study of the celestial motions and the *correct* interpretation of their terrestrial effects."

In 1950, not so long after Nelson had begun his observations, and well before the publication of his findings, the young French statistician Michel Gauquelin initiated a long investigation that was to produce intriguing results.

Statistical analysis

Gauquelin set out with the intention of proving that there was *no* correlation between planetary positions at a person's birth and his or her future development. He had some previous investigations to consider: the famous psychologist Carl Gustav Jung had begun a rather superficial analysis of the astrological relationships of married couples, which he had abandoned; Karl Ernst Krafft, the Swiss once rumored to have been Hitler's private astrologer, had put together a vast accumulation of miscellaneous data; and the French astrologer Paul Choisnard had claimed to have discovered relationships between the aspects of Mars in the natal horoscopes of soldiers, between Mercury and Moon

in the nativities of philosophers, between Sun and Moon in those of celebrities, as well as between Sun and Mars in cases of premature death.

Gauquelin began by investigating the natal horoscopes of some 25,000 subjects, and he was soon able to state with confidence that there appeared to

In every case, there was a correlation between the position of certain planets at birth and the subject's career.

be little justification in the claims made by Krafft and Choisnard. He looked then at a piece of research by another French astrologer, Leon Lasson, who claimed a significant correlation between Mars and the ascendants of 134 politicians, between Venus and the ascendants of 190 artists, and between Mercury and the ascendants of 209 actors and writers.

Medical men

When Gauquelin put his data to this test, he was amazed that he obtained the same results. With a sample of 576 eminent professors of medicine, he discovered that a high proportion had been born just after Mars or Saturn had risen or passed the MC. In a group of 508 leading doctors, he obtained a similar relationship, and he calculated that the odds against this being a matter of chance were a million to one.

Puzzled, Gauquelin assembled data from all over France for eminent soldiers, politicians, writers, sportsmen, and clerics; in every case, there was a correlation between the position of certain planets at birth and the subject's career.

The Great Fire
This woodcut from a broadsheet published by the astrologer William Lilly in 1664 shows the sign of Gemini (associated with London) being consumed by fire.

Michel Gauquelin

And even more surprisingly, these results applied only to those who were successful in their careers. For instance, in a group of 1,458 scientists who had never won a prize or made any important discovery, Gauquelin found that there was no statistical significance in the position of Mars, Saturn, or Jupiter in the horoscope.

Official skepticism

When Gauquelin published his findings, the French popular press took a great deal of interest in them, but other scientists refused to comment. Eventually, Jean Porte of the Institute of Statistics replied that the findings applied only to France, and therefore revealed some aspect of the national character that had nothing to do with astrology. Then Marcel Boll, a member of a committee of Belgian scientists set up specifically to study paranormal phenomena, commented: "Your conclusions are nothing but pulp-romances....If you undertook the same inquiry in Britain, Germany, the U.S.A. or Russia you would come out with nothing but national idiosyncracies."

Warlike Mars

Stung, Gauquelin set out with his wife to collect data from birth registers in Germany, Italy, Holland, and Belgium; and in due course he found the results

he compiled were comparable to those he had found in France, but with some interesting variations. For instance, Mars appeared for Italian soldiers significantly more often than for Germans. He suggested that, as was well-known, Germans are far more warlike as a nation than Italians, and that one would therefore expect German soldiers to be far less in need of a strong Martian influence in their horoscopes in order to be successful.

Statistical significance

Altogether, the Gauquelins assembled birth data for more than 25,000 people. In the horoscopes of 3,305 scientists, Mars was found in one or other of the significant positions 666 times, where the statistical average would have been 551 — and the odds against this were 500,000 to one. In the horoscopes of 3,142 military leaders, the planets Mars and Jupiter occurred in these positions in 640 cases, compared with an average of 524 — the odds against this being a million to one.

It was also found that significantly low figures were obtained for planetary positions in certain groups. Actors, painters, writers, and musicians, for instance, showed an unusually low frequency of the planets Mars and Saturn in important positions in their natal horoscopes.

Gauquelin published further details of his research in *The Truth About Astrology* (1984). He had also looked for any correlation with the position of the sun in the horoscope, but could find nothing of statistical significance. However, other researchers in the U.S.A. and Britain followed up his work.

In America, Edward van Deussen collected 163,953 birth-dates for individuals born in the U.S.A. and

Zodiacal man
This illustration is from an English astrological work of the late 14th century. It shows the signs of the zodiac associated with the different parts of the body.

THE BLACK GAME

Both sides in the Second World War used psychological warfare. Even the ancient art of astrology was employed to help confuse and demoralize the enemy.

*I*N SPRING 1937 A ROMANIAN named Virgil Tilea was in Zurich with his wife and there met Karl Ernst Krafft, who cast Tilea's horoscope. Tilea was impressed by the reading, and even more so the following year when Krafft made some accurate predictions about prominent Romanians. In January 1939 Tilea was appointed to the Romanian legation in London. Krafft wrote to him, offering to draw up a more detailed horoscope. The letter, though mailed from Bucharest, was written in Berlin. Tilea realized that Krafft must be close to the Nazi hierarchy, and told British intelligence.

Strategically valuable

He suggested to them that Krafft was making predictions for Hitler and his associates, and that it would be strategically valuable to employ an astrologer in London who could make the same predictions. He proposed a man named Louis de Wohl.

By autumn 1940 de Wohl had been hired by the Psychological Warfare Executive (PWE). In May 1941 he was sent to America to disseminate subversive astrological predictions so that they would be published and eventually reach Germany. De Wohl drew up the horoscopes of various Nazi leaders, and told journalists what misfortunes they were about to suffer.

The Führer's astrologers

In August 1941 de Wohl read a paper to the American Federation of Scientific Astrologers, stating that Hitler was advised by "the best astrologers in Germany." He said that the Russian offensive was: "the first major action of Hitler which could not have been counter-signed by his astrologers." He also forecast that Hitler planned to attack the U.S.A.

Virgil Tilea

Louis de Wohl
De Wohl was a prominent astrologer who helped in the preparation of forged astrological documents for British intelligence during the Second World War.

Meanwhile Rudolf Hess, Hitler's deputy, had fled Germany on May 10, 1941, and flown to Scotland. The Nazis put out a story that Hess had been disastrously influenced by astrologers, and the Gestapo began to round up all the practitioners of astrology that they could find. On June 12 Krafft was arrested, but nobody in British intelligence knew of this.

Forged documents

When de Wohl returned to Britain in the autumn, he was asked to help PWE produce forged astrological documents (under the direction of the journalist Sefton Delmer). These were then smuggled into occupied France and from there found their way into Germany.

Ellic Howe, who supervised the printing of these documents, has described some of them in his book *The Black Game* (1982). There was the "Brandt-Rasputin booklet," which contained a forgery of Krafft's handwriting, and the statement that it was a copy of one of his letters to Hitler. This was followed by "21 pages of glorious nonsense," suggesting that the influence of Dr. Karl Brandt, one of the Führer's physicians, was as evil as that of Rasputin. But the letter was dated November 14, 1943, and by then Krafft had already been in a Gestapo prison for 18 months.

Probably more effective were the issues of *Der Zenit*, a tiny astrological magazine targeted at U-boat crews. This suggested that the submarines should not be sent to sea on "unfavorable" days. This publication was attributed to the astrologer Dr. Hubert Korsch — PWE being unaware that he too had been in the Gestapo's hands for nearly two years.

Astrological accuracy

Delmer and Howe confessed in their memoirs that, much as they had enjoyed their work, they had little idea of how effective these documents had been in terms of psychological warfare. But years later Howe learned that another astrologer, Wilhelm Wulff, had escaped the clutches of the Gestapo and had been Himmler's personal astrologer in the last months of the war. Wulff had been summoned by the head of the Criminal Police, shown a copy of *Der Zenit*, and asked to assess how accurate it was.

Der Zenit
The bogus astrological magazine produced by the British Psychological Warfare Executive during the Second World War. It was intended principally to demoralize German U-boat crews.

Rudolf Hess

Dr. Alan Smithers
Dr. Smithers, of the University of Bradford, England, collaborated with a sociologist, Joe Cooper, in a major statistical survey into the relationship between birth-date and career. The project involved well over 35,000 subjects, and broadly confirmed that in many cases there was a correlation between what time of year a person was born and the type of work he or she did.

Canada. In Britain sociologist Joe Cooper, in association with Dr. Alan Smithers of the University of Bradford, collected another 35,000 birth-dates. Between them, these various researchers reported the following findings:

◆ Out of 28,000 soldiers, a significantly high proportion were born in late summer or early autumn, with peaks in Leo and Scorpio.
◆ 6,412 doctors showed above-average figures for births in summer and autumn.
◆ Out of 8,932 musicians, an above-average number were born in winter or early spring, with the sun in Sagittarius, Capricorn, Aquarius, or Pisces.
◆ 6,677 American lawyers showed a peak in Gemini.
◆ British politicians peaked in Aries.
◆ 7,118 advertising agents and 1,834 diplomats peaked in Gemini.
◆ Out of 5,056 schoolteachers, a significant proportion were born with the sun in Leo or Virgo.
◆ 5,111 librarians showed a marked trend to Libra.
◆ Out of 3,927 authors, a high proportion had the sun in Virgo.
◆ There was a marked tendency for comedians' birthdays to fall in the spring — in Aquarius, Pisces, Taurus, or Gemini.

Shortly after these figures had been published, a group of British doctors published their analysis of 28,000 patients born between 1921 and 1955 who were admitted to psychiatric care in 1970–71. They said that 7 percent more manic depressives and 9 percent more schizophrenics than average were born in January, February, or March.

A nervous disposition
In 1977, Jeff Mayo, a professional astrologer, and Professor Hans Eysenck, an eminent psychologist, collaborated in

an investigation of another claim made by astrologers: that people born in Cancer, Scorpio, or Pisces tend to be overemotional or neurotic. They reportedly found that those born with the sun in the even-numbered signs — Aries, Gemini, Leo, Libra, Sagittarius,

---

People born in Cancer, Scorpio, or Pisces tend to be overemotional or neurotic.

---

and Aquarius — tended to be extroverts; while those born with the sun in the other signs showed introvert tendencies. And they showed that Cancer, Scorpio, and Pisces (and, to Mayo's surprise, Aries) were statistically linked with emotional or neurotic personality traits.

Professor Hans Eysenck

Marital bliss
One of Eysenck's colleagues, Beverley Steffert, investigated the belief that there was a connection between astrological sun signs and happy marriages. She found that successful marriages are more likely when both partners are born in either even-numbered or odd-numbered signs.
Whether the positions of the planets provoke changes in gravitational or magnetic fields, or induce showers of high cosmic radiation, and whether these influences have a profound (and predictable) effect upon those about to be born, requires a great deal more serious research. But it begins to seem that we have underestimated the ancients, and that the magicians of Babylon might have known more about the forces of destiny than the scientists of the modern world have been prepared to give them credit for.

THE JUPITER EFFECT

A vital clue to predicting violent and dangerous geological upheavals may lie in the stars.

*I*N THEIR BOOK *The Jupiter Effect* (1977) John Gribbin and Stephen Plagemann put together a theory that connected the positions of the planets with the occurrence of earthquakes. Jupiter and Saturn come into conjunction every 20 years or so: seen from Earth they were in conjunction from November 1980 to March 1981, and again in August 1981, while in relation to the Sun they were in conjunction in May 1981.

Gribbin and Plagemann predicted that this latter conjunction would be accompanied by the lining up of nearly all planets on one side of the sun. The American writer Arthur Prieditis predicted "world-shattering political upheavals of the first magnitude" accompanying disastrous earthquakes. Subsequently, Gribbin withdrew his prediction of earthquakes, when more mature calculations showed that the lining-up of the planets would not occur in May 1981.

Gribbin also speculated that "the San Andreas Fault...might be triggered in the later 1970's or early 1980's, shortly after the next period of maximum solar activity." He eventually settled on spring 1982 for this event. There was no earthquake at this time; however, it is interesting to note that, at the time of the San Francisco earthquake of October 18, 1989, Saturn, Uranus, and Neptune were close together on one side of the Sun. Jupiter was very nearly directly opposite them, and Mars was square to them.

Cataclysm in California

At the time of the great San Francisco earthquake of 1906, there was a similar planetary aspect. Jupiter, Neptune, Mars, and Venus were close to conjunction, with Saturn square to them. Further research is needed to establish whether there is indeed any real connection between planetary alignments and geological upheaval on earth.

Jupiter and Saturn
This early 16th-century German book illustration shows the planets Jupiter and Saturn in a stressful, dangerous aspect. They are in direct opposition, that is, in Taurus and Scorpio respectively. These planets were also in opposition during the San Francisco earthquake of October 18, 1989.

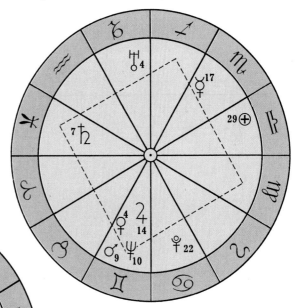

Zodiacal chart for the first San Francisco earthquake on April 18, 1906

Zodiacal chart for the second San Francisco earthquake on October 18, 1989

Earth's horoscope
These two charts show the position of the earth at the time of the two major San Francisco earthquakes. The earth is represented by the symbol ⊕. In 1906 the earth was at 29 degrees Libra. In 1989 it was at 26 degrees Aries. In both these charts the sun is at the center.

ASTROLOGERS TO THE THRONE

Throughout the ages, and right up to the present day, kings, emperors, and statesmen have put their faith in astrologers to forecast coming events.

DR. JOHN DEE

A near-contemporary of Nostradamus was the English mathematician Dr. John Dee. He was born just outside London in 1527, and at 19 was teaching Greek at Trinity College, Cambridge.

Dee traveled widely in Europe, and in about 1550 he began to take an interest in astrology and other aspects of magic. Queen Mary I asked him to cast horoscopes for herself and her prospective bridegroom, Philip of Spain. Unwisely, Dee also drew up the horoscope of Mary's half-sister, the future queen Elizabeth. (This has been preserved in the British Museum.) He was accused of treason and then acquitted, but remained in prison until 1555.

Royal patronage

In 1558, when Mary died and Elizabeth succeeded her, the new queen asked Dee to determine a propitious date for her coronation; and from then on he remained close to the throne. It is said that Elizabeth consulted with Dee on the very day she died in 1603.

Dee, however, gained a reputation for being involved in black magic, and his house was wrecked by a mob. Luckily they spared his "magic glass" — the crystal sphere he used for his divinations, which can also be seen today in the British Museum.

*I*N ANCIENT ROME, LITTLE WAS DONE without the advice of an astrologer. For he not only gave his prognostications on the progress of a war, the founding of a city, or the succession of a king or emperor; he also calculated the portents for a marriage, a journey, or a move to a new house.

But Rome fell, and the secrets of astrology were lost — except to the followers of Muhammad, who found the manuscripts of Ptolemy, the greatest of Egyptian astronomers, in the library at Alexandria. For 600 years the Arabs studied science and mathematics, and preserved the teachings of the astrologers. Yet it was not until the 13th century, when European scholars were invited to Toledo in Spain to study at the great library established there by the Moors, that this wisdom became once more available to the West.

A self-fulfilling prophecy

One of these European scholars was a cleric called Michael Scot from the Scottish Borders town of Balwearie. He was the tutor of the young Frederick II, king of Sicily and subsequently Holy Roman Emperor, and in 1220 was appointed court astrologer. The 14th-century writings of Francesco Pipini tell the story of Scot predicting his own death. He determined that he would be killed by a small stone of a certain weight, and so invented a special protective covering for his head. But during Mass one day he removed this at the most sacred part of the service, and a small stone fell from the vault of the church and hit him on the head. Scot weighed the stone — it was exactly the predicted weight. He immediately put his affairs in order and left for his birthplace in Scotland. There he died of the wound, and is said to be buried in Melrose Abbey.

Royal family horoscopes

Perhaps the most famous royal astrologer of all is Michel de Nostredame (known as Nostradamus), born at St. Rémy, France, on December 14, 1503. In 1555 he published the first part of his verse prophecies, and the following year he was summoned to the royal court in Paris. There he was asked to cast horoscopes for the queen's children. Soon after, he returned to Provence, but in 1565 one of these children, the young king Charles IX, appointed him "doctor and counselor in ordinary to the king." Nostradamus did not have long to enjoy royal favor, as he died the following year.

During the next two centuries astrology declined in Europe, but interest revived in the late 19th century. In Germany, astrology became associated with a trend in

> "An astrologer just picks the best time to do something that someone else has already planned to do. It's like being in the ocean: you should go with the waves, not against them."
>
> **Joan Quigley**

metaphysical thought that was adopted by the Nazis. In the 1920's several diviners drew up horoscopes for the emerging leader of the party, Adolf Hitler — including German astrologer Elsbeth Ebertin.

"A man of action born on 20 April 1889, with Sun in 29 degrees Aries," she wrote in 1923, "can expose himself to personal danger by excessively incautious action, and could very likely trigger off an uncontrollable crisis. His constellations show that this man is to be taken very seriously indeed; he is destined to play a *Führer-role* in future battles."

This prediction increased interest in astrology among the Nazi Party. The only Nazi leader known to have employed an astrologer is Heinrich Himmler, but Goebbels also took an interest, realizing its propaganda value.

President protection

In recent years, several public figures have admitted to being influenced by astrology. One of these is Nancy Reagan. According to her memoirs, *My Turn* (1989), she regularly consulted Californian astrologer Joan Quigley during her husband's presidency.

Mrs. Reagan would telephone Quigley with the President's schedule in front of her and ask whether specific dates were safe or dangerous. Then she would call Michael Deaver, who was in charge of the schedule, and try to make small changes according to the astrologer's advice.

When Donald Regan, the White House chief of staff, published his own revelations about Mrs. Reagan's reliance upon astrology, there was a major scandal. "Astrologer Runs the White House" blared the headlines in the *New York Post*. But as Joan Quigley put it in an interview with *Time*: "An astrologer just picks the best time to do something that someone else has already planned to do. It's like being in the ocean: you should go with the waves, not against them."

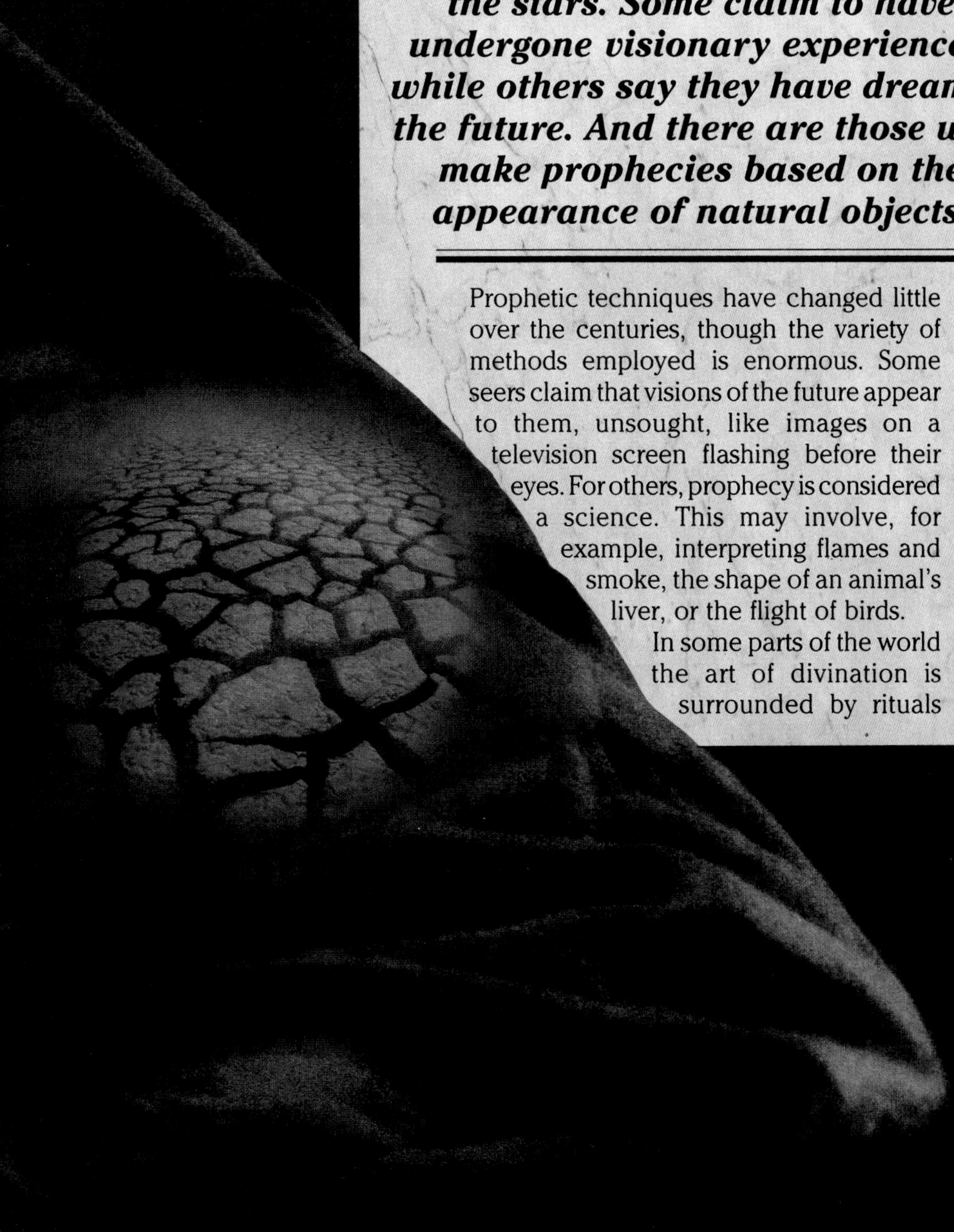

CHAPTER THREE

PROPHETIC REVELATIONS

Not all diviners read the future in the stars. Some claim to have undergone visionary experiences, while others say they have dreamed the future. And there are those who make prophecies based on the appearance of natural objects.

Prophetic techniques have changed little over the centuries, though the variety of methods employed is enormous. Some seers claim that visions of the future appear to them, unsought, like images on a television screen flashing before their eyes. For others, prophecy is considered a science. This may involve, for example, interpreting flames and smoke, the shape of an animal's liver, or the flight of birds.

In some parts of the world the art of divination is surrounded by rituals

Pcora moziemtur et peribunt.

qmultū mel r lymza   Infantes moziemtur.
brt.

njel hūnrabit   r parū lmī.
Karitas lmū.

I: Amte apłor pctri i paulū.I:Ahi affūpaonē

The year in pictures
This page is from a 14th-century English illuminated manuscript that predicted events over a seven-year period. The text is in Latin and elaborates on the information in the pictures. This fragment foretells that livestock will die (a cow and a sheep on their backs); children will die (two children in bed); flax will be scarce and costly (a few bundles of flax), and honey will be plentiful (many beehives). The important fast days of the year are represented by the images at the bottom of the page.

intended to bestow special powers on the diviner, shaman, priest, or priestess. Often these practices involve entering a trance state, and the actual prophecy appears to come from some supernatural source, such as a god, goddess, or spirit.

The will of the gods
The purpose of divination in the ancient world was to discover the will of the gods. This reflects the fatalism of early religions. The Sumerians and Babylonians believed that everything that happened to men and animals was a portent, and it was the priest's job to interpret these events. By 3000 B.C., the Sumerians — who lived in the area that today is Iraq — had evolved a staggeringly complex array of divinatory techniques, ranging from interpretation

of dreams and the movement of animals to the direction of the winds and deformities in children. The study of a liver from a sacrificed animal was an important method of divination — unusual bumps and formations on the organ were interpreted by the priest as good or evil omens.

The sacred art
The Sumerians used these techniques both for personal concerns and for important matters of state. The diviners of the Etruscan civilization in ancient

> The study of the liver of a sacrificed animal was an important method of divination — unusual bumps and formations on the organ were interpreted by the priest as good or evil omens.

Italy used animal entrails to foretell the future. Both the Etruscans and the Mayas of Mexico held the role of the diviner-priest as sacred, and considered his prognostications to represent no less than the destiny of his people.

The oracle at Delphi
Divination played a significant role in daily life in the ancient Mediterranean region, and Greece in particular was noted for its oracles. Although Dodona in northwest Greece was the first prophetic center, the most famous was at Delphi, just north of the Gulf of Corinth.

Legend had it that the Delphic oracle was founded by the god Apollo on the site of an ancient temple, located in a naturally occurring amphitheater, at the foot of Mount Parnassus. Zeus, the king of the gods, declared this place to be the center of the world.

The priestess through whom the oracle spoke, known as the Pythia, had to be past child-bearing age. She would seat herself on a tripod after elaborate purification rites and wait for questions.

FALSE PROPHECIES?

Skeptics argue that all prophets are false, and all prophecies are hoaxes. But people tend to believe what they want to believe, and false prophecies are surprisingly difficult to uncover.

IT IS RELATIVELY EASY TO FOOL PEOPLE into believing that you can foresee the future. You only need to know a little about human psychology and choose your words well. Just say that someone important will soon arrive on the scene, that there is danger on the horizon, and care should be taken over a health condition. The "client" will do the rest. That seems to be the philosophy of many fortune tellers who have earned lucrative livings as self-styled seers. Some mediums and others wo claim to possess psychic powers are also known to use "cold reading" to glean information from the people who consult them. This involves picking up clues from the appearance, manner, and speech of the client to find out more about him or her and then feeding this information back to the client in ways that seem impressive.

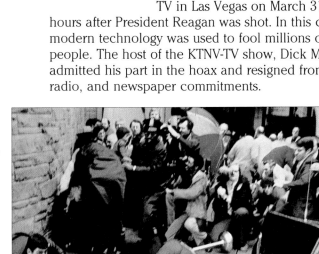

Jeane Dixon

Fortune-telling experiments

It is also fairly easy to give a reading that appears specific yet is so general that almost anyone will recognize characteristics that they believe apply exclusively to them. In fact, recent research with students, all of whom were given identical readings in a dream analysis test, showed that the majority felt that the information related directly to them. Further experiments were conducted in which conflicting data was given to another group of students. They also thought many points were applicable to themselves. As the research continued, it became obvious that most individuals were able to identify characteristics in almost any reading given to them. This may be why so many people are convinced that an analysis applies specifically to them.

Hedging your bets

Some psychics phrase their predictions in such a way that they can claim success no matter what the outcome. Famous Washington seer Jeane Dixon, for example, was asked about the impending American presidential election when she appeared on "A.M. San Francisco" on April 11, 1984. She replied that Walter Mondale would become the Democratic candidate "unless the people change their thoughts." And who would win? Ronald Reagan, she said, "unless they change an awful lot and switch at the last moment."

On April 2, 1981 – four days after an assassination attempt on President Reagan by John Hinckley – NBC-TV's "Today" show and ABC-TV's "Good Morning America," as well as Cable News Network, showed a video recording of Los Angeles psychic Tamara Rand apparently predicting the event beforehand.

A shooting foreseen

Rand said Reagan would be shot in the chest by a sandy-haired young man from a wealthy family with the initials "J.H." She believed his first name would be Jack and his surname something like "Humley." Rand said there would be a "hail of bullets" and the attack was likely to happen in the last week of March or the first week of April.

Subsequent investigation, however, showed that the tape had not been broadcast for the first time on March 28, at WTBS in Atlanta, Georgia, as Rand had claimed. It had, in fact, been recorded at KTNV-TV in Las Vegas on March 31, 24 hours after President Reagan was shot. In this case modern technology was used to fool millions of people. The host of the KTNV-TV show, Dick Maurice, admitted his part in the hoax and resigned from his TV, radio, and newspaper commitments.

Assassination attempt
On March 30, 1981, John Hinckley gunned down President Reagan. Both San Francisco astrologer Joan Quigley and Los Angeles psychic Tamara Rand claimed to have foreseen this. It was later proven beyond doubt that Rand's prediction was made after the event.

The Pythia at Delphi
A 19th-century view of the priestess in a visionary trance.

THE MISLEADING ORACLE
Croesus, king of Lydia from 560 B.C. to 546 B.C., consulted the Delphic oracle about whether or not to attack Cyrus the Great of Persia. The oracle told him that he would destroy a mighty empire if he did so. Next Croesus asked how long his kingdom would last. The answer was: "Until a mule is monarch of Media." Croesus's third question was about his deaf-and-dumb son. The oracle replied that it would be a bad day for Croesus when his son spoke.

First words
Croesus prepared an army and invaded Persia. He was driven back and finally defeated at the siege of Sardis. A Persian soldier attacked Croesus, not knowing who he was. The shock of seeing his father in mortal danger prompted Croesus's son to call out: "Do not kill Croesus."

The oracle's meaning now became clear. A mighty empire had indeed fallen: that of Croesus himself. It had indeed been a bad day for Croesus when he had heard his son speak. Cyrus, the Persian emperor, was also king of Media, and was in fact of mixed parentage – metaphorically speaking, a "mule."

The person who consulted her would present a cake and sacrifice a sheep or goat before being able to consult the oracle. The Pythia was said to be speaking on behalf of the god Zeus and her reply would usually be incomprehensible. Priests, however, were on hand to interpret the god's meaning, most often in the form of verse.

Predictive verses
At the peak of the Delphic oracle's popularity, two Pythias were used, and a third was held in reserve. The inquirers ranged from kings and emperors to humble people.

The answers were usually presented in bad verse and ambiguously phrased. In time such flawed responses undermined the reputation of all oracles. At the same time, Greek political factions began to use the Delphic oracle for their own purposes

> As the Romans became more sophisticated and Christianity's influence spread, divination declined.

and the temple at the site was looted, burned down, and rebuilt. The oracle was consulted more and more about trivia, and after the 4th century A.D. there are no further records of it.

The mighty and the humble
The Egyptian god Amon was also thought to speak through oracles. Amon's oracle center in the Libyan desert kept in touch with the oracle of Zeus at Dodona by using doves to carry messages between them.

The Romans also had official prophets, numerous oracles, and various magicians and soothsayers, of whom Spurinna is the best known. He warned Julius Caesar of his impending death on the ides of March. Apollonius of Tyana,

who was born in Asia Minor around 4 B.C., was known as a fortune teller throughout the Roman Empire. He gave away his possessions and lived in poverty so that he could wander from temple to temple giving advice, preaching and healing the sick.

Cicero's book *On Divination* (written around 45 B.C.) supported the use of augury (divination by omens) for reasons of state but rejected all other forms of divination. This hypocrisy can be explained by the fact that Cicero had held the office of augur since 53 B.C. As the Romans became more sophisticated and Christianity's influence spread, divination slipped into decline.

Prophetic *Centuries*
In the Middle Ages, however, prophecy enjoyed a revival. In 1556 the French seer Nostradamus was summoned to court by Catherine de Médicis to explain a prediction concerning the death of a French king, made a year earlier in his *Centuries*. After the prophecy was tragically fulfilled with the death of Catherine's husband, Henry II, Nostradamus returned to court to predict the destinies of her seven children.

In the same century, English occultist John Dee acted as philosopher

Amon
The Egyptian god of fertility was thought to speak through an oracle. This silver and gold statue of Amon dates from c. 900 B.C.

and adviser to Queen Elizabeth I. His knowledge of future events was said to come from peering into the depths of a crystal the size of an egg. There were many others probing the boundaries between science and the occult in those days, but their achievements were largely eclipsed by the Age of Reason and the growing materialism of the 18th and 19th centuries.

Modern believers

Yet now, in the 20th century, we find belief in prophecy almost as widespread as it was 2,000 years ago. Many of the early techniques are still employed and even people holding high office are known to consult those who profess to be capable of foretelling the future. The results of a Gallup Poll on the paranormal in the U.S. (conducted in June 1990) showed that a quarter of the population believed in astrology and 26 percent "in clairvoyance, or the power of the mind to know the past and predict the future."

Are the believers just gullible? Or have they, too, been given a glimpse of tomorrow which has convinced them that the future can be seen?

Cicero the augur
The Roman author and orator Marcus Tullius Cicero wrote a book in favor of augury. He recommended that it be used to give guidance in affairs of state.

THE BRAHAN SEER

The gloomy visions of a Highland Scot baffled his 17th-century contemporaries. But after his death many of his prophecies became reality.

ALTHOUGH THE prophecies of Kenneth Odhar – known as the Brahan Seer – were largely confined to his native Scotland, where he lived and worked as a farm laborer in the 17th century, his fame has spread far afield. Most often he predicted gloom and bloodshed, which he did with relish in his native Gaelic. The prophecies were handed down from generation to generation by the families mentioned in them, or their enemies.

Many of his long-term predictions seemed unlikely at the time, but his reputation for accuracy has kept interest in him alive – and some of his visions have apparently been fulfilled in recent years.

The 3rd earl of Seaforth

Stained with Highland blood

Once, when walking across a bleak moorland, the seer predicted to his companion that before many generations passed the moor would be "stained with the best blood of the Highlands." In 1746 – 116 years after Odhar's prophecy – the Battle of Culloden, the result of the last Jacobite uprising, took place at that very spot. The cream of Bonnie Prince Charlie's force of 5,000 Highlanders – Camerons, Frasers, Macdonalds, Macintoshes, and Stewarts – died there.

Among the other predictions he made were that "strings of black carriages, horseless and bridleless" led by "a fiery chariot" would pass through the Highlands. That must have bewildered the Scots 400

Countess Isabella, wife of the 3rd earl

years ago – but the introduction of the steam train in Victorian times fits the description perfectly. Just as puzzling was his claim that ships with sails would pass behind Tomnahurich, a hill near Inverness. When the Caledonian Canal opened in the 1820's that is exactly what happened.

A magic stone

Odhar lived on the Isle of Lewis and his gift was attributed to a magic stone which is said to have been given to him either by fairies or a ghost (the stories differ). In time he was released from his labors to become the personal seer of the Seaforth family, whose home was Brahan Castle. His patron, the earl of Seaforth, was sent to Paris in the 1660's by King Charles II, and failed to write to his wife, the Countess Isabella, for many months. So she asked Odhar what he was doing. He replied that the earl was happy and, when pressed, explained that he was "on his knees before a fair lady."

The Brahan Seer seems not to have foreseen what would happen next, for the countess ordered him to be burned to death in a tar barrel as a witch. The sentence was carried out – but not before Odhar predicted how the great Seaforth family would die out. He prophesied that the last chief would be born deaf and dumb and outlive his four sons. The prophecy was fulfilled in every detail when Francis Humberstone Mackenzie died in January 1815.

Black rains

As for Odhar's still unfulfilled prophecies, many wonder about his claim that men would return from other countries to work in the Highlands when the "horrid black rains" fall. It has been suggested that this might refer to the discovery of offshore oil, or to a calamity (possibly nuclear) yet to occur. Only time will tell.

APOCALYPSE NOW?

The end of the world has been forecast many times. Fortunately the specific nature of these predictions has so far been matched only by their inaccuracy.

Elizabeth Prophet
As head of the Church Universal Triumphant, Prophet persuaded the 2,000 members that the world would end on April 23, 1990. On that day her followers took to an underground network of shelters they had built on a 30,000-acre site in the northern Rocky Mountains. The day passed just like any other.

The prophet Zoroaster
A central principle of the Zoroastrian religion is the apocalypse, when the earth will be purged by fire and the Wise Lord, Ohrmazd, will triumph over his evil opponent, Ahriman.

O N FEBRUARY 5, 1962, the world held its breath. Indian astrologers had announced that on this day all the planets would be in conjunction in Capricorn and this would destroy the earth. Indian holy men led a mass prayer session lasting nine days. Half a million pilgrims immersed themselves in the holy river Ganges. Nothing happened.

The end of time

In 1843 farmer William Miller from New York state announced that, by his calculations, based on the Book of Daniel, the world would end "sometime between March 21, 1843, and March 21, 1844."

Thousands of people along the eastern seaboard put their faith in Miller's prediction, and money was raised for a tabernacle to be built in Boston. When March 21, 1844, came and went, a new date was announced: October 22, 1844. Miller's followers became more fervent in their belief. They even left their crops standing in the field at harvest time. On the appointed day, one man put on a pair of turkey wings, climbed a tree and begged the Lord to take him up. He fell and broke an arm. Otherwise, the day passed without incident.

History is full of such stories. Humankind is fascinated by attempts to foretell how, and especially when, the world will end. Constant disappointments

The approach of the second millennium after the birth of Christ has fueled all kinds of apocalyptic speculation.

seem not to have dispelled enthusiasm for the subject, and in modern times the approach of the second millennium after the birth of Christ has fueled all kinds of apocalyptic speculation.

The teachings of Zoroaster

The word "apocalypse" comes from the Greek word *apokalypsis* which means "unveiling" or "disclosure." Apocalyptic cults focus on revelations, often cryptic, about God's sudden, cataclysmic intervention in the affairs of man. The teachings of Zoroaster, who founded the religion of Zoroastrianism in the 6th century B.C. in Persia (modern-day Iran), are the likely

Earth under threat
The earth cannot last forever. But the nature and timing of the final cataclysm have been the subject of some lively debate over the centuries.

PROPHETIC REVELATIONS

THE END OF THE WORLD

There is one prediction that we can make with some certainty: one day the world will end. Our earth cannot outlast the sun, and the sun is slowly dying. Estimates vary, but there is a general consensus that we only have another 4.5 billion years of sunshine left.

An optimistic note

Jack Hills, an astrophysicist at Michigan State University, made a more optimistic prediction in 1979. He said that the earth would be swallowed up by an enormous "black hole." This is an extremely dense invisible body with an enormous gravitational field that sucks in everything, including light itself. The hopeful note in his forecast was that this was not likely to happen for another 25 billion years.

The vulnerable earth

Unfortunately, we are still vulnerable. At any time, the earth could be obliterated by a supernova (an exploding star). Or we could be hit by an asteroid or a comet. In this case, no amount of preparation — underground shelters, food stores, etc. — will save us from destruction.

John of Patmos
This late 15th-century painting shows John (known as "the Theologist") dictating to a scribe. He is passing on a divine message from Jesus Christ. This has been recorded as the last book of the New Testament, The Revelation to John.

origin of the apocalyptic literature that was developed further by Judaic, Christian, and Islamic writers.

The best known of these writings is the last book of the New Testament, The Revelation to John. This is written as if related from God to Jesus Christ, and then, in turn, to his disciple, John, who was living in exile on the island of Patmos in the Aegean Sea, just off the coast of Turkey. John could well have been a historical figure whose prominence, during a period of open conflict between the church and the Roman state in the late A.D. 80's, led to his banishment to the island. It is known that, near Ephesus in Turkey, within 10 or 20 years of the fall of Jerusalem in A.D. 70, a prophetic group was formed and led by a man named John.

Encouraging the faithful

In Revelation, Christ appears to give John authority as his prophet to the church. Scholars assure us, however, that this two-part book is a collection of writings from different authors who lived during the last quarter of the 1st century A.D. It is likely that the Roman persecutions of that period inspired much of the work, which is designed to give reassurance to Christian followers that God would eventually triumph over his enemies, and to encourage them to

The first horseman of the apocalypse
This late 14th-century representation shows the apocalyptic figure of Pestilence, described in Revelation 6:2: "And I saw, and behold, a white horse, and its rider had a bow; and a crown was given to him, and he went out conquering and to conquer."

Many people have confidently predicted major global confrontation between good and evil as the 20th century draws to a close.

remain steadfast in their faith. It is a message that is meant to apply not only to those days but to future times when other Christians would also face persecution.

Visions of catastrophe

The first part of Revelation is really a moral discourse, devoid of visions and symbolism, taking the form of seven letters from Christ through John to seven churches in the Roman province of Asia, and ending with a message for the whole church. The rest of the book is full of symbols, visions of catastrophe, references to Satan, martyrs, and the victory of the Archangel Michael. False prophets are described as beasts who bring destruction to the unfaithful. Another beast, usually referred to as the Antichrist, is mentioned: this is a man, signified by the number "666." Many people believe that this referred to the Roman emperor, Nero.

Victory over the Antichrist

What is unusual is that, unlike previous apocalyptic literature, which was cryptic and vague in its meaning, Revelation was written to give a clear prophecy about the times in which it was produced. It also gives a clear prediction about the end of time, when God will triumph in his judgment over the harlot Babylon (Rome) and Christ will achieve victory over the Antichrist and his followers. Nevertheless, it

contains a number of allegories and unexplained symbols that leave it open to widely varying interpretation.

In the final chapter we learn of the thousand-year reign of Christ and the defeat of Satan and the beasts by a fire from heaven. This last judgment, although cataclysmic, will lead, we are told, to a new heaven and a new earth: the new Jerusalem.

So when will this great event occur? The references to "a thousand years" have led many self-styled prophets and seers to attach particular significance to the years A.D. 1000 and A.D. 2000.

The year A.D. 1000, however, passed comparatively quietly. But many people have confidently predicted major global confrontation between good and evil as the 20th century draws to a close.

The Day of Judgment
This 16th-century allegorical painting is from the school of Martin de Vos. It shows the orb of the world enchained by Death and a demon. A sinner sits on the left, and a redeemed man is crowned on the right.

THE PROPHECIES OF NOSTRADAMUS

Did Nostradamus's psychic vision really penetrate the mists of future centuries to see the career of Napoleon, the rise of Hitler and the deaths of the Kennedy brothers? The answers to these questions really depend on the way you interpret the Centuries, *the 942 rhymed verses that contain his prophecies.*

ICHEL DE NOSTREDAME was born at St. Rémy, Provence, France, on December 14, 1503. His family converted from Judaism to Catholicism when he was nine. In 1522, he began to study medicine in Montpellier and became well known for his treatment of the plague, about which he wrote a book. Ironically, his wife and two children died of the plague in 1538.

Nostradamus, as he was known, was a scientist who appears to have had no interest in the occult in his early days, although his study of astronomy would certainly have included astrology. He may have had, some supporters believe, psychic powers. On a visit to Italy in the late 1540's, for example, Nostradamus is reported to have addressed a young monk, Felice Peretti, as "Your Holiness." Over 35 years later, and nearly 20 years after Nostradamus's death, Peretti became Pope Sixtus V.

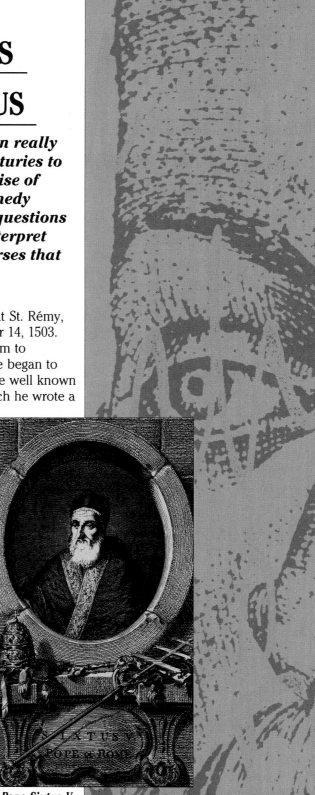

Pope Sixtus V

The *Centuries*

Nostradamus owes his reputation as a seer to his almanac of prophecies, called the *Centuries*, the first part of which was published in Lyons in 1555. These were four-line rhyming verses (quatrains) arranged in groups of a hundred. These prophecies apparently came to Nostradamus in the form of divinely inspired clairvoyant visions.

In his introduction to the *Centuries*, Nostradamus explains that "so as not to upset my present readers I would do this in a cloudy manner with abstruse and twisted sentences, rather than the plain prophetical." In *They Saw Tomorrow* (1977) one of the seer's 20th-century supporters, Charles N. Gattey, agrees that "the language is enigmatic, at times almost unintelligible, as if written in code. The verses are not in chronological

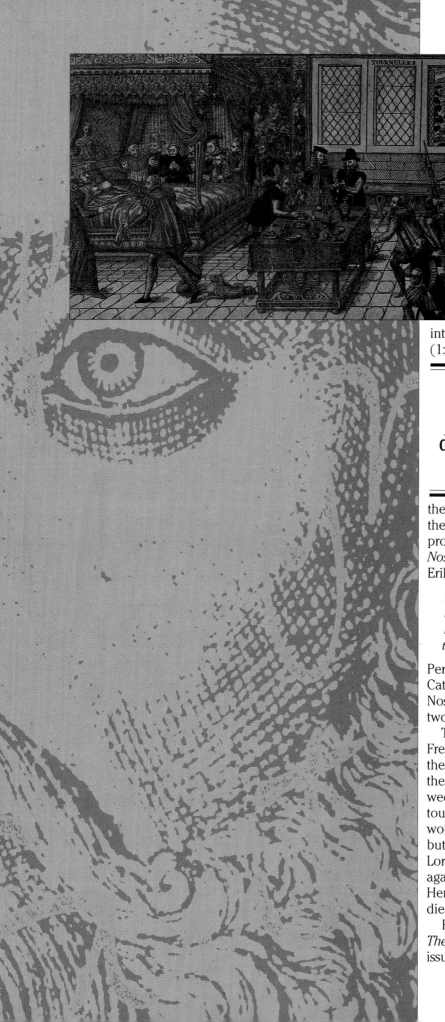

A royal tragedy
Scene at the deathbed of Henry II,
mortally wounded in a joust.

order, and jump about in time and subject." He adds: "Everywhere we find mystifying puns and anagrams." Also, the quatrains are written in a polyglot of French, Provençal, Italian, Greek, and Latin. Even in Nostradamus's own day, scholars had difficulty in making sense of his prophecies. But some seemed clearer than others.

In the first "Century," an interpretation of one of the quatrains (1:35) appeared to predict the death of

Even in Nostradamus's own day, scholars had difficulty in making sense of his prophecies.

the king of France in a duel. (This and the following translations of the prophecies are from *The Prophecies of Nostradamus* [Perigee Books, 1973], by Erika Cheetham.)

> *The young lion will overcome the older one,*
> *in a field of combat in a single fight:*
> *He will pierce his eyes in their golden cage;*
> *two wounds in one, then he dies a cruel death.*

Perturbed about this prophecy, Queen Catherine de Médicis ordered Nostradamus to court, and granted him a two-hour audience on August 16, 1556.

Three years after Nostradamus met the French queen, in the summer of 1559, there were three days of celebrations at the royal court, following a double wedding, ending with a series of tournaments. The French king, Henry II, won all his jousts on the first two days but on the third day the lance of Gabriel Lorges, count de Montgomery, splintered against the king's; the point penetrated Henry's visor and pierced his eye. He died 10 days later in agony.

Researcher James Randi, writing in *The Skeptical Inquirer* of Fall 1982, takes issue with the assumption that this

The death of a king
One of Nostradamus's prophecies has been interpreted as applying to the execution of the English king Charles I on January 30, 1649. This painting of the scene is by 19th-century artist Ernest Crofts.

The arrest of a king
In June, 1791, Louis XVI tried to escape the horrific consequences of the French Revolution by fleeing France. His arrest at Varennes appears to have been foretold in detail over 200 years earlier in the Centuries.

quatrain has anything to do with the death of the king. He points out that Henry's helmet was not made of gold; the king was the older by only a few years; neither knight used the lion in their heraldic crests; and that there was only one wound, not two. He says the word "wounds" was added in later editions of the work — from 1568 onward — in an attempt to make the quatrain fit the events. The earlier translation of this word was "knells," which in this context appears to make little obvious sense.

The fate of another French king, Louis XVI, is said to have been predicted in quatrain 9:20:

> *By night will come through the forest of Reins two partners,*
> *by a roundabout way; the Queen, the white stone.*
> *The monk-King dressed in gray at Varennes*
> *the Elected Capet causes tempest, fire and bloody slicing.*

This could refer to the French Revolution and the flight of the king (disguised in a monastic robe according to some accounts) and Marie Antoinette from Paris in 1791. What is remarkable is that Nostradamus names the town — Varennes — where they were captured. "Bloody slicing" is believed to be a reference

to the guillotine. Some writers claim that in another quatrain (9:34) Nostradamus even names the man in whose house the king and his wife stayed after their arrest at Varennes: M. Saulce.

Napoleon's women
Another quatrain (4:54) mentions a man "of a name which was never borne by a French king," adding: "there was never so fearful a thunderbolt. Italy, Spain and the English tremble. He will be greatly attentive to foreign women." That, say the believers, undoubtedly refers to Napoleon Bonaparte, who took the title of emperor of France and terrorized Europe early in the 19th century. He had two wives, a Creole and an Austrian, as well as a Polish mistress.

Nostradamus's prophecies dealt with other countries too. Quatrain 8:37 has been translated:

> *The fortress near the Thames will fall*
> *when the king is locked up inside.*
> *He will be seen in his shirt near the bridge,*
> *one facing death then barred inside the fortress.*

A clear reference, some say, to the English king Charles I's imprisonment in Windsor Castle and subsequent execution in a white shirt.

Turning his attention to Germany, the French seer predicted in quatrain 2:24:

> *Beasts wild with hunger will cross the rivers,*
> *the greater part of the battle will be against Hitler.*
> *He will cause great men to be dragged in a cage of iron,*
> *when the son of Germany obeys no law.*

Many believe that this is a remarkable prophecy. But the original has the name in the second line as "Hister," which is also an old name for the River Danube. Hitler himself and other members of the Third Reich, notably Goebbels, who became Minister of Propaganda, took a keen interest in the writings of Nostradamus. We can only wonder to what extent the influence of such prophecies can make them self-fulfilling.

What do we make of quatrain 2:6?:

Near the harbour and in two cities
will be two scourges, the like of which have never been seen.
Hunger, plague within, people thrown out by the sword
will cry for help from the great immortal God.

It could certainly refer to the atomic bomb attacks on Hiroshima and Nagasaki in Japan in 1945. But it might describe equally well the aftermath of any major modern war.

We can expect a string of calamities before the century ends.

So what does Nostradamus predict for us in the future? Erika Cheetham writes in *Further Prophecies of Nostradamus* (Perigee Books, 1985): "Nostradamus regarded Hitler as the second antichrist, Napoleon being the first, and the third is to descend upon us all in the late 1980's." She goes on to say that in quatrain 2:46 the French seer suggests a link between a comet, the outbreak of the Third World War, and the inevitable advent of the third Antichrist:

After great misery for mankind an even greater approaches
when the great cycle of the centuries is renewed.
It will rain blood, milk, famine, war and disease.
In the sky will be seen a fire, dragging a trail of sparks.

Another of Nostradamus's quatrains (10:72) prophesies:

In the year 1999, and seven months,
From the sky will come the great King of Terror
He will bring back to life the great king of the Mongols
Before and after War reigns happily.

Nostradamus indicates in other verses that the third Antichrist will come from the Euphrates region (present-day Iraq or Iran). Believers have been keeping an eye on this region for signs of an emerging evil leader. Both Ayatollah Khomeini of Iran and Saddam Hussein of Iraq have been suggested as candidates. Apparently we can expect a string of calamities before the century ends.

Interpretation through hindsight

Most of Nostradamus's prophecies are so vague and timeless that they could be taken to mean anything. They can be "understood" only with hindsight. For example, quatrain 10:66 reads:

There will be a head of London from the government of America
He will tempt the Island of Scotland by a trick
They will have Reb for King, a very false Antichrist
Who will put them all in confusion.

This is one of the few specific references in the *Centuries* to America, which had only recently been discovered in Nostradamus's time. No commentators have been able to make convincing sense of this prediction. Believers suggest that the reason for this is simple: it hasn't happened yet!

There is no shortage of quatrains that have been interpreted as referring to the U.S.A. "The world put into trouble by three brothers; their enemies will seize the marine city, hunger, fire, blood, plague, all evils doubled" has been seen as a chilling presentiment of the troubles of the Kennedy family. "Earthshaking fire will cause tremors around the New City" is supposed to refer to a cataclysm engulfing New York City.

But these interpretations tend to stretch the credibility of the serious researcher. The skeptics' view is summed up by David Pitt Francis, author of *Nostradamus: Prophecies of Present Times?* (1984). In Pitt Francis's opinion, the French seer's success is not due to his prophetic powers but solely to "the ingenuity of interpreters."

Nagasaki, September 1945
The quatrain that has been assumed by some authorities to predict the atomic bomb attacks on Hiroshima and Nagasaki at the end of the Second World War could equally well apply to any number of wartime devastations in recent centuries.

Saddam Hussein
This warlike ruler of Iraq has been suggested as a candidate for the role of third Antichrist, predicted by Nostradamus in the 16th century.

INTERPRETING NATURE

Augury is the interpretation of natural objects and events to foretell the future. If you feel nervous when a black cat crosses your path, you are participating in a human tradition at least 5,000 years old.

THE SUMERIANS, WHO LIVED IN what is now Iraq 3,000 years B.C., developed a variety of divination methods that they believed revealed the will of God. Their principal method was augury: the interpreting of omens in nature. In his book, *Amulets and Superstitions* (1930), Sir E. A. Wallis Budge, former keeper of Egyptian and Assyrian antiquities at the British Museum, explains:

"The priests derived omens from dreams...from the planets and stars, from eclipses, from the movements of animals, from the flight of birds, from the appearance of snakes at certain places, from locusts, lions, the actions of dogs, the direction of the winds, the state of the rivers, from peculiarities of newly-born children and animals, from the birth of twins, from accidents...from deformities in children, from the birth of monstrosities, from the symptoms which occur in diseases, etc. According to the Sumerians and Babylonians everything that happened to the king, and to men and animals and birds and reptiles, portended something, and the priest was expected to tell the enquirer what that something was."

A scientific approach

The priests adopted an orderly approach in their work, keeping records of events and modifying their methods in an attempt to improve their accuracy. A favored technique was haruspicy — divination by examining the entrails of animals. The theory behind this was that an animal, when consecrated and sacrificed, passed from the domain of humans to that of the gods. The gods were thought to show their disposition during the sacrifice, and particularly in the appearance of the bodily parts of the sacrificed animal — usually the liver.

Biblical evidence

Evidence of haruspicy goes back at least as far as Sumerian and Babylonian times. A passage in the Bible (Ezekiel 21:21) tells us: "For the king of Babylon stands at the parting of the way, at the head of the two ways, to use divination; he shakes the arrows...he looks at the liver." Clay models of livers that were used for training novices have also been found, inscribed in both Babylonian and Hittite.

Consulting animals' entrails was also practiced by the Greeks and Romans, both of whom used Etruscan soothsayers as expert consultants on the subject. The Romans even had state officials, called augurs, who

The future in nature
Our ancient ancestors devised many systems of foretelling the future. These were based on almost every sort of natural event, from the flight of birds to the shape of a flame.

RHABDOMANCY

The use of rods, wands, or pendulums to find subterranean water or hidden treasure is known as rhabdomancy, or dowsing. The miracle of Moses at Meribah, causing water to flow by striking his rod against a rock (Exodus 17:4 – 6 and Numbers 20:8 – 12), has been cited as the first historical reference to this remarkable power. But there may be an earlier reference in an African rock painting in caves near Tassili, north Sahara, dating from c. 6000 B.C. This appears to show a cattle herder walking behind his animals, holding a forked stick in the way that today's dowsers do.

Moses
The biblical prophet used a rod to locate water for the people of Israel.

Modern dowsing

In modern times, science has not been able to explain the phenomenon; but rhabdomancy has become a respectable profession nevertheless. Dowsers regularly save their clients thousands of dollars by finding the location and depth of subterranean substances such as water, oil, and minerals. They may even do this using a pendulum swinging over a map, without actually visiting the location.

Sexing a baby

Experienced dowsers claim that they can determine the sex of an unborn child by holding a pendulum over the mother's womb. They start by letting it swing back and forth "in neutral" and then mentally ask what sex the child will be. The pendulum's swing will then change and each dowser learns from experience how to interpret its gyrations to answer the question correctly. Clockwise rotation usually indicates a male, and counterclockwise a female.

made pronouncements on such natural phenomena as thunder and lightning, the movements of birds and animals, and freak weather. Roman armies took sacred chickens with them when they marched, and studied how they ate. If they gobbled their food the omens were good.

Another method of foretelling the future, favored particularly by North American Indians, involved a circle of written prophecies and a knife. The knife would be spun by the person wanting to know the future. All was revealed when the point of the knife came to rest. Like the Romans, the Greeks were also eager to read divine intent into thunder and lightning, as well as the flight and song of birds. In ancient Greece, even a sneeze was believed to have special meaning.

Many of these ancient divination techniques have been handed down over the centuries and continue to be practiced, in one form or another, today. Every civilization has had a belief in at least some form of divining the future.

Shamans on the island of Madagascar draw circles on the ground, then drop seeds into them. The patterns formed give them the answers to their questions. Witch doctors in some parts of Africa allow a crab to scrabble around in a bowl of wet sand. They then read fortunes by interpreting the marks that the crab has made.

Another age-old technique is pyromancy — the use of fire for divination. As wood or coal burns, the patterns produced slowly change and it is possible to see images in the glowing embers. In Western society, various shapes came to have special meanings. Large circles were interpreted as a good omen for a marriage, but double rings warned that a hasty marriage might fail.

Many of the symbols in the shapes are self-evident: a hatchet indicated bad luck, a shoe promised that good news was on its way, and a four-leaf clover meant great prosperity and success. But most of the shapes remained a matter of personal interpretation.

Divining by water

The use of water as a focus for divinatory powers — hydromancy — was another widespread method of prognostication. In its simplest form it involved studying one's reflection. If this was clear then so, too, would be the days ahead. But a broken or disturbed image was supposed to be an omen of trouble. Other reflective surfaces, such as bronze and silver mirrors, were used by the Romans, Greeks, and Egyptians.

When glass mirrors were introduced in the 13th century, it was not long before they too were used for prophecy.

Animal augurs
In late classical times, fortune tellers used hens in their divinations. This hen is spelling out a message by pecking at grains of food set next to letters of the Greek alphabet arranged in a circle.

Mirror divination — called catoptromancy — was used as a predictor of health, and also to find missing people or treasure. Even in modern times, the tradition has persisted that a girl will see the reflection of her future husband over her left shoulder if she looks into a mirror at midnight on Halloween.

Tibetan augury

One of the esoteric arts of Tibet is divination by *tra*, a type of augury. The diviner focuses on a mirror, or the calm surface of a lake, or the sky. He concentrates on the question and then empties his mind, usually by reciting mantras, until a vision appears. In *Divination and Oracles* (1981), the researchers M. Loewe and C. Blacker describe a particular instance of the use of *tra*. A woman in East Tibet consulted a diviner about how many sons she would have. The diviner used a mirror and had a vision of three flowers: one red, one yellow, and one slightly damaged white one. He explained to the woman that she would have three sons: one would be a reincarnate *lama*, or high priest, one would be a monk, and one would not enter the religious life, and be subject to ill-health. All of the diviner's prophecies, according to the authors, duly came to pass.

Scientific skepticism

It is difficult to account for the continuing popularity of these techniques of augury in the face of scientific skepticism. It is hard to believe that they work; but if they do not work, why have they remained so popular over thousands of years? The reason may have nothing to do with prophetic powers.

What all these techniques have in common is that they introduce the element of

chance. Such a concept, for early man, might well have been a life-saver. For if he found animals in a certain direction on one hunt, it was likely that he would return to the same spot next time. Yet in time the game would move elsewhere, either in search of food, or out of fear of further attacks. Thus if primitive man had continued to return to the same spot, he would have starved. Instead, it is possible that he used some random-selection technique to point him in a completely new and untried direction.

It may not always have led him to his next meal, but it might have caused him to question habits formed from past experience, so that he sought new and better hunting grounds. This theory might help explain the strength of human interest in augury and divination.

> In ancient Greece, even a sneeze was held to have special meaning.

Looking in the liver
This Roman relief is from Ostia in Italy, and dates from the 3rd century A.D. It shows a haruspex — an augur specializing in telling the future from the appearance of the entrails of certain animals.

Bamboo basics
A fortune teller from the Kachhi region of Pakistan divines the future with the aid of a few bamboo poles.

SECRETS OF THE AUGURS

Ancient man probably started using techniques of augury and divination to direct him to food sources. Whether they worked or not, the methods multiplied through the ages, and were used by many cultures in many different parts of the world. Some of these techniques, with very little change, have survived to the present day.

Navajo sand painting
The Navajo Indians create intricate works of art using sands of many different colors. The medicine men of the tribe also used colored sands in a type of geomantic divination. They would let the sands trickle through the fingers to create patterns on the ground, and then interpret their significance.

Geomancy
The art of geomancy is one of the oldest means of divination and is widespread around the world. It involves casting objects such as sticks, stones, or colored sands to make a pattern, or making holes apparently at random upon a map or a figure drawn on the ground, and then interpreting the arrangement of the objects or the marks to foretell the future.

Pointers of fate

Belomancy
Babylonian priests practiced divination by arrows. There were usually just two — marked with signs meaning "yes" and "no." They were shuffled and a blind selection was made to give a response to a question. A third arrow was sometimes added; its sign meant "don't know" or "do as you like."

African diviner
This Senufo diviner from the Ivory Coast in Africa
uses a turtle shell containing cowrie shells, seeds,
and small bronze figurines. He throws these on the
ground to make his divination. In the background is a
clay pot full of water, tree sap, and leaves; this is for
the devil to bathe in. The diviner is assisted by a pair
of small ancestral figures that he has placed in front
of the mirror.

African
divining
tablets
These divining
tablets and their
protective cases were
used to tell the future
by shamans of the
Mashona tribe of Zimbabwe
in southern Africa.

SHAMANS
For centuries primitive tribes
around the world have sought a
glimpse of the future through a
shaman — a medicine man, priest,
or medium. Through contact with
the spirit world the shaman is
believed to be able to heal the
sick and solve other problems.

Although the word derives from
the Russian/Tungus language of
Siberia, shamanism is a worldwide
phenomenon. It still flourishes in
Siberia, Korea, Tibet, Malaysia,
Thailand, Africa, Australia, and
among the Eskimos of Hudson
Bay. Its rituals and beliefs are
strikingly similar wherever they
are found.

These include knowledge of
helpful spirits, the memory of
certain myths and shaman-songs,
the rules for sacrifices and rituals,
and shamanic paraphernalia such
as drums, costumes, and mirrors.

Inherited powers
Many shamans inherit their
special powers, others discover
them by accident, and a few feel a
calling. Whatever the path that

leads an individual into
shamanism, he or she has to
undergo an initiation that,
although regarded as a spiritual
experience, is frequently painful.
The initiate's personality may
change, becoming moody or
aggressive, and occasionally there
is self-mutilation or even suicide.
The initiation is supposed to
involve a period of contact with
spirits, demons, and
lost souls in the
next world.

Altered
consciousness
The shaman's power is based on
altered states of consciousness.
These can be induced by
drumming, chanting, fasting, or
sensory deprivation. Another
method is the use of drugs made
from hallucinogenic plants, such as
peyote, jimson weed, and certain
types of mushrooms. By using such
techniques and ingesting such
substances, the shaman enters into
a trance in which he can visit
either heaven or hell.

Sudanese
shaman
*This witch
doctor from the
Azande tribe of
Sudan, in Africa, is
holding a rodent's
skull in his mouth
while he casts a spell.*

Cover of Fate *magazine, June 1955*

Crystallomancy

This method is better known as crystal-gazing or scrying. The seer interprets visions he or she claims to see in a sphere or ovoid of glass, crystal, beryl, or similar precious stone.

Tea leaves

In recent centuries, a popular method of divination has been to study the residue left by tea leaves and/or coffee grounds. The patterns in the bottom of the cup are interpreted as shapes that show the future.

Training model

Looking at livers

This clay model of a sheep's liver was used to train Roman students in the esoteric science of haruspicy. Its surface is divided into 55 sections, reflecting the divisions of heaven; discolorations or deformities in any part of the liver had a particular meaning — favorable or unfavorable. A variation on this method was ichthyomancy — the examination of fish entrails to divine the future.

A promising pattern?

Man in the moon?

Catoptromancy, or mirror-gazing
Young girls used to predict when they would be married by looking at the moon's reflection in a mirror. They calculated how many years they had to wait by timing how many minutes it took before a bird or a cloud crossed the lunar face.

Etruscan diviner

Haruspicy
This Etruscan bronze of about the 5th century B.C. shows a priest examining the entrails of an animal. This ancient art was known as haruspicy. It involved divination from the detailed examination of a liver, or other internal organ, from a sacrificed beast. Etruscan priests were entrusted with the sacred duty of charting the fate of the nation, and relied heavily on this technique to give them guidance.

A death foretold

Ceromancy
This 19th-century satirical cartoon lampoons the gullibility of superstitious people. The divination technique shown here is ceromancy, which is based on the shapes made by the melted wax from a candle. In this case the shape is like a funeral winding sheet — causing great consternation to the watchers.

Pyromancy
In its simplest form this involved interpreting images in burning embers or in the flames of a fire, or burning substances such as eggs, flour, or incense, and interpreting shapes in the smoke. Some cultures interpreted the shape of a candle flame. A curling spiral of flame, for example, was thought to give a warning of enemy plots. An ancient English tradition called for maidens to place a nut among hot embers; if it jumped, their romance would be a success.

Flickering fortunes

DREAMS OF THE FUTURE

Can some people tune into startling depictions of future events in their dreams? Several eminent personalities have claimed to have this frightening power, dreaming of the future exactly as it subsequently occurred. And there are those who claim to have used this same ability for recreational and even lucrative ends.

FOR TEN CONSECUTIVE NIGHTS, a 23-year-old office manager in Cincinnati, Ohio, had a recurring nightmare. In his dream he heard an aircraft's engines failing and then watched as a huge three-engined American Airlines airplane swerved sharply in the air, rolled over and crashed to the ground. His dream premonition was so real that he heard the terrible explosion and felt the searing heat of the mass of red and orange flames. Each night, David Booth woke up in horror; the nightmare haunting him throughout his waking hours. It was, he said, unlike a dream. "It was like I was standing there watching the whole thing — like watching television."

Worst disaster in history

He was so troubled by this experience that he decided to take action. On Tuesday, May 22, 1979, he telephoned American Airlines, the Federal Aviation Authority (FAA) at the Greater Cincinnati Airport, and a psychiatrist at the University of Cincinnati. Although they treated his calls sympathetically there was little they could do. Four days later, on the evening of May 26, 1979, an American Airlines DC-10 crashed as it took off from Chicago's O'Hare International Airport; 273 people died. It was the worst disaster in the U.S.A.'s aviation history.

The FAA's public affairs officer Jack Barker described the dream premonition as "uncanny," adding: "There were differences, but there were many similarities. The greatest similarity was his calling [naming] the airline and the airplane...and that [it] came in inverted." He revealed that the FAA had made every possible effort to match up the details of David Booth's nightmare with a known airport or airplane but it was not until the crash actually happened that all the details fell into place.

A preventable accident?

What would have happened if they had been able to identify the plane and the airport? Could David

A mixed blessing

It may sound like a useful skill to be able to dream of the future. But some people find themselves dreaming the same horrifying dream again and again, night after night — with the conviction that the tragedy is just about to happen.

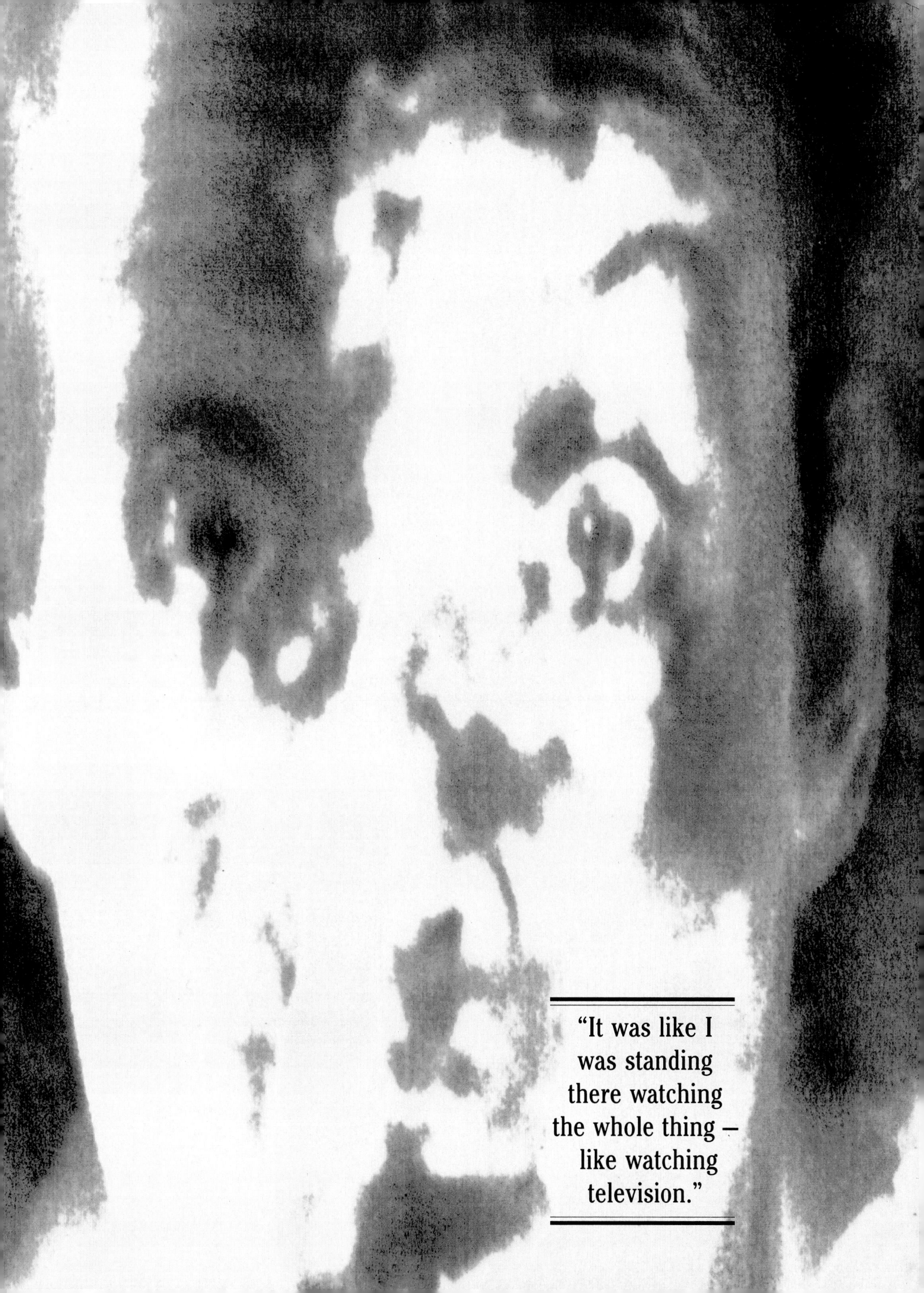

"It was like I
was standing
there watching
the whole thing —
like watching
television."

LOOKING FOR TROUBLE
Dr. John Barker, an English psychiatrist, conducted a survey into premonitions of the 1966 Aberfan disaster, in which a coal waste tip engulfed a village school in Wales. His research convinced him that precognitive dreams were a reliable indicator of forthcoming disasters. He proposed an initiative whereby this type of information could be gathered, analyzed by computer, and used to avert similar major tragedies in the future.

Premonitions bureaux
In 1967 the British Premonitions Bureau was set up in London by Peter Fairley, the science correspondent of the *Evening Standard* newspaper. People were invited to send in premonitions, which were date-stamped, filed, and compared with later events. The bureau gathered a large amount of data, none of which could be considered as conclusive proof of the reliability of premonitions. The bureau subsequently closed down.

The American Society for Psychical Research in New York has opened a file on dreams and premonitions, and currently welcomes information on cases from the general public.

Booth's premonition actually have prevented the accident?

People usually have premonitions about their own lives or of those near and dear to them. One puzzling aspect of David Booth's dream of the DC-10 disaster is that he does not appear to have had a connection with anyone involved in the crash. Why did he glimpse those particular moments in the future? No one can answer for certain.

Assassination!
President Abraham Lincoln had a vivid dream on an April night in 1865. He dreamt that he was awakened by sobbing and got up from his bed in the White House and followed the sound. He found himself in the East Room where people were filing past a catafalque. Men and women were paying their last respects to a figure lying in state, guarded by soldiers. The face was covered, so he asked one of the guards who had died. "The President," the

> **People usually have premonitions about their own lives or those of individuals near and dear to them.**

soldier replied. "He was killed by an assassin." The group around the catafalque gave a loud cry of grief and Lincoln awoke. The President told his wife, Mary, and several friends about the troubling dream. That same month the prophecy was tragically fulfilled when the President was assassinated at Ford's Theater by John Wilkes Booth.

War crime
The political assassination that led to the First World War appeared in a dream recorded by Bishop Dr. Joseph Lanyi, former tutor of Archduke Francis Ferdinand of Austria. The bishop was at Grosswardein, Hungary, and the Archduke 300 miles away at Sarajevo, in Bosnia-Hercegovina, on June 28, 1914, when a dreadful dream woke Lanyi at 3.15 A.M. He dreamed he had gone to his desk early in the morning and found a black-bordered letter with a black seal and the arms of the Archduke. He recognized Francis Ferdinand's writing and saw at the top of the letter a small blue picture, like a postcard, depicting the Archduke and his wife in a car, accompanied by a general and an officer. Crowds lined the street, waving and cheering. Suddenly two young lads leapt forward and shot at the car.

In his dream Lanyi read the text of the letter, which said: "Dear Dr. Lanyi, Your Excellency, I wish to inform you that my wife and I were the victims of a political

Abraham Lincoln

ABERFAN

In 1966 catastrophe struck a tiny village in Wales as the local school was engulfed in a landslide. Many people claimed to have foreseen the event, some in terrifying detail.

A NINE-YEAR-OLD WELSH GIRL, Eryl Mai Jones, insisted that her mother listen to details of her dream. "I dreamt I went to school and there was no school there! Something black had come down all over it," she explained. Next day, October 21, 1966, 144 people were killed when a half-a-million-ton coal waste tip, made unstable by heavy rain, fell onto the village of Aberfan, burying the school and other buildings. Eryl was one of 128 children who perished in the disaster.

It soon became apparent that Eryl's dream premonition was just one of many that seemed to have foreshadowed the catastrophe. Some were experienced by those whose lives were to be affected by the tragedy; others had no obvious connection with the people or the place.

A woman in Sidcup, London, told two friends seven days before the tragedy: "I had a horrible, vivid dream of a terrible disaster in a coal mining village. It was in a valley with a big building filled with children. Mountains of coal and water were rushing down the valley, burying the building. The screams of the children were so vivid that I screamed myself."

Avalanche of coal
Another woman had a vision while in a Spiritualist church at Plymouth, Devon, 200 miles away from Aberfan, on the evening before the catastrophe. "First, I saw an old school house nestling in a valley, then a Welsh miner, then an avalanche of coal hurtling down a mountainside. At the bottom of this mountain of hurtling coal was a little boy with a long fringe looking absolutely terrified to death. Then for quite a while I saw rescue operations taking place. I had an impression that the little boy was left behind and saved. He looked so grief-stricken. I could never forget him, and also with him was one of the rescuers wearing an unusual peaked cap." She claimed to have seen the same boy and the rescuer later in television coverage of the accident.

Genuine premonitions
A London psychiatrist, Dr. John Barker, appealed for reports of similar cases. He was convinced that 60 of the 76 cases he received — mostly from the London area — were genuine, and apparently succeeded in confirming 24 of them through independent witnesses.

The scene of the Aberfan disaster

Dream premonitions accounted for 36 of the original cases; the rest were waking visions or feelings of unease. He noticed that the premonitions gradually built up in the week preceding the tragedy, reaching their peak the night before the disaster.

Collectively, the premonitions Dr. Barker analyzed gave the name of the village or a name strikingly similar (in three cases), the date on which it occurred, the fact that a massive coaltip was involved, and that a school would be engulfed, suffocating many children.

Sweet dreams?
A subject has her sleep patterns monitored at the Maimonides Medical Center.

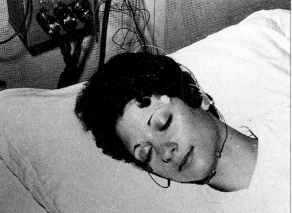

DREAM LABORATORY

In the 1960's Dr. Montague Ullman, a psychiatrist and parapsychologist, conducted extensive research into the nature of dreams at the Maimonides Medical Center in New York. Dr. Ullman and his colleague, Dr. Stanley Krippner, devised an experiment to test for precognition that would eliminate the possibility of any other sort of ESP experience such as telepathy or clairvoyance. For this they enlisted the help of British psychic Malcolm Bessent.

An unpleasant charade

On the first night, Bessent had four dreams, which were kept secret from the research team. The following day, Dr. Krippner chose the word "corridor" at random, and the associated painting by Van Gogh, "Hospital Corridor at Saint Rémy." The team then subjected Bessent to an unpleasant charade involving his captivity in a mental hospital, complete with white-jacketed medical personnel and distant hysterical laughter. The intention was to give Bessent an emotional experience which, it was hoped, his dreams might have forecast.

The experience foretold

Bessent then revealed that his dreams had involved a mental hospital, doctors in white coats, and a female patient trying to escape down a corridor toward an archway.

These dreams had occurred before the key word and the painting had been selected, and before the following day's drama had been devised. The close correlation appeared to be more than might be explained by coincidence.

assassination. We recommend ourselves to your prayers. Cordial greetings from your Archduke Franz, Sarajevo, June 28th, 3:15 A.M." Lanyi wrote down exactly what he had dreamed and said Mass immediately for the couple. He told his servant, his mother, and a guest what he had dreamed. Confirmation that it was true came in a telegram at 3:30 P.M.

But only one assassin was responsible for the assassination — not two as Lanyi had dreamed. This weakens the case for those who have attributed this event to clairvoyance. Discounting pure coincidence, of course, the incident might be attributable to another form of paranormal activity: telepathic exchange between the Archduke and Lanyi — the Archduke may not have had time to see who was shooting at him.

Steamboat pilot

It is impossible to explain the experience of Samuel Clemens — better known in later life as the writer Mark Twain (1835–1910) — in terms of telepathy. Before he became a writer he worked as an apprentice pilot on the *Pennsylvania* steamboat on the Mississippi River, alongside his younger brother Henry, a clerk. While visiting a sister in St. Louis, Sam had a vivid dream in which he saw a metal coffin, containing the body of his brother, resting on two chairs. A bouquet of white flowers, with a crimson one in the middle, had been placed on his chest.

Following an argument with the chief pilot of his boat a few days later, Sam was transferred to another boat, the *Lacey*. Henry stayed behind. When Sam's boat reached Greenville, Mississippi, he learned that the

Pennsylvania had blown up just outside Memphis and 150 had perished. His brother survived the blast but was badly scalded, and Sam spent six days and nights with him until he died.

When Sam went to pay his last respects, the scene that greeted him was exactly as he had seen it in his dream — with one exception. Henry was in a metal coffin resting on two chairs, but there were no flowers. Yet as Sam looked down at his brother an elderly woman entered the room. She placed a bouquet of white flowers, with a single crimson one in the center, on Henry's body, then left.

Once in a lifetime

Such dreams are usually once-in-a-lifetime experiences, which leads skeptics to dismiss them as chance occurrences. After all, we have dream periods on average between three and five times a night, amounting to a total of 90 minutes. Because one dream often

Mark Twain
The American writer is only one of many creative artists to have reported psychic experiences of one sort or another. Are they more sensitive than ordinary people to this sort of phenomenon? Or more imaginative? Or merely more likely to express it if or when it happens?

merges into another, it is estimated that we may each have ten dreams a night, whether we remember them or not. Small wonder, then, that every now and then one of those dreams will bear a resemblance to a future event.

Picking winners

A really useful premonitory dream was reported by the journalist John Godley — later Lord Kilbracken — in the *Journal of the Society for Psychical Research* in June-July 1947. Godley dreamed in March of that year that he was looking at the next day's evening newspaper open at the racing results! On waking, however, he could remember just two winners: Bindal and Juladin. He put money on the two horses and won. He decided to keep a pencil and paper by his bed to record other dreams but they all proved rather ordinary until, on April 4, he again dreamed of seeing the winners in a newspaper. This time he remembered only one: Tubermore. No such horse existed so he put his money on a similar-sounding horse, Tuberose, which romped home.

In one dream he found himself in a telephone box talking to his bookmaker's clerk about the last race. He dreamt that the clerk told him that the winner was Monumentor at 5-4. The horse nearest to this name in the final race was Mentores. He backed it and it won at 6-4.

Similar dreams followed and Godley even gave two tips to an English national newspaper, the *Daily Mirror*. They both won and the *Mirror* carried a two-page story about him on June 18,

Lord Kilbracken

> ## Godley dreamed that he was looking at the next day's evening newspaper, open at the racing results!

1947. He later joined the newspaper as a racing journalist. Not all his subsequent dreams were successful, however.

Godley registered with the Society for Psychical Research his predicted winner of the 1972 Grand National — Neat Turn — but no horse of that name was entered. Godley suggested that his growing knowledge of racing had interfered with the dream process.

Dream machine

To prove that dreams might open doors to the future, there needs to be some way of controlling them to produce a repeatable experiment. Dr. Keith Hearne is an English psychologist who has researched lucid dreaming. This most commonly occurs in the semi-conscious state just before a sleeper wakes up, when he or she feels able to control events in the dream. Dr. Hearne invented a "dream machine" to help people recall their dreams. It works by monitoring the sleeper's breathing rate, which often increases during dreaming, triggering an alarm to awaken the sleeper after a variable delay.

Dr. Hearne conducted a survey of 88 people who had reported dream premonitions. His research revealed a sexual bias — nine out of ten were female — and that a third of all his respondents had experienced between ten and 50 premonitions. A fifth estimated their total to be over 50! "Clearly, premonitions are not isolated phenomena occurring randomly in the population," he concludes. "They seem to concentrate in certain people."

Richard Newton

A PROBABLE PREDICTION

Richard Newton, a teacher from Gloucester, Massachusetts, made a brave prediction just before Christmas 1978. Both in writing and on television, he forecast that on March 11 the following year there would be a plane crash. He said that a plane with a red logo on the tail would crash just outside a city in the northern hemisphere, and 45 people would be killed.

Sure enough, he was almost exactly right. On March 14, 1979, a Royal Jordanian Airlines jet crashed at Ad Dawhah, Qatar, in the Persian Gulf. Forty-seven people were killed.

Beware the ides of March

Newton denied being psychic. He had simply researched plane-crash statistics in a book called *Destination Disaster* (1976) and made a prediction based on probability. He discovered that very few planes fly in the southern hemisphere. Most crashes happen on takeoff or landing, and so occur near cities. More than half the world's commercial jets have some red on their tails. The most dangerous month to fly is March, and the second week — the ides of March — is the most hazardous. And finally, the average number of deaths in a plane crash is 45.

THE MEANING OF DREAMS

The fantasy world of our dreams has often fascinated and frightened the human race. Some of our ancestors believed in a dream world they could visit at night and regarded the events there as just as real as those in the waking world. Others believed dreams were messages from the gods — usually warnings about the future.

SLEEP AND THE NATURE OF DREAMS, are still something of a mystery, though our knowledge of both has grown with the introduction of modern scientific methods of monitoring sleep states. In 1953, for example, a young physiologist at the University of Chicago named Eugene Aserinsky discovered that our eyes move rapidly when we dream. This sleep state is known as REM (rapid eye movement) and it has enabled researchers to pinpoint a period of dreaming and to awaken sleeping subjects immediately when it finishes, so that they can describe their experiences.

The art of interpretation

But what do our dreams mean? One of the earliest attempts at dream analysis was Artemidorus's treatise, *The Interpretation of Dreams*, of the 2nd century A.D. Over the centuries the art of dream interpretation has changed with our growing awareness of the nature of the human psyche.

Freud and Jung were collaborators at one point but eventually the two came to interpret dreams differently. Freud used the technique of free association to develop his psychoanalytical method while Jung evolved the concepts of extroverted and introverted personalities, archetypes, and the collective unconscious. Jung also disagreed with Freud's belief that there was a direct or indirect sexual basis to almost every image.

Flying in dreams

In *Dream Worlds* (1976), the author Stuart Holroyd explores the extent of this divergence of view by considering the different interpretations each gave to the experience of flying in dreams. Freud believed that flying was a symbol of sexual activity, since the gliding and hovering could produce pleasurable sensations comparable to those of sex. Jung, on the other hand, saw flying in dreams as a symbol of escape from mundane matters, of freedom and transcendence.

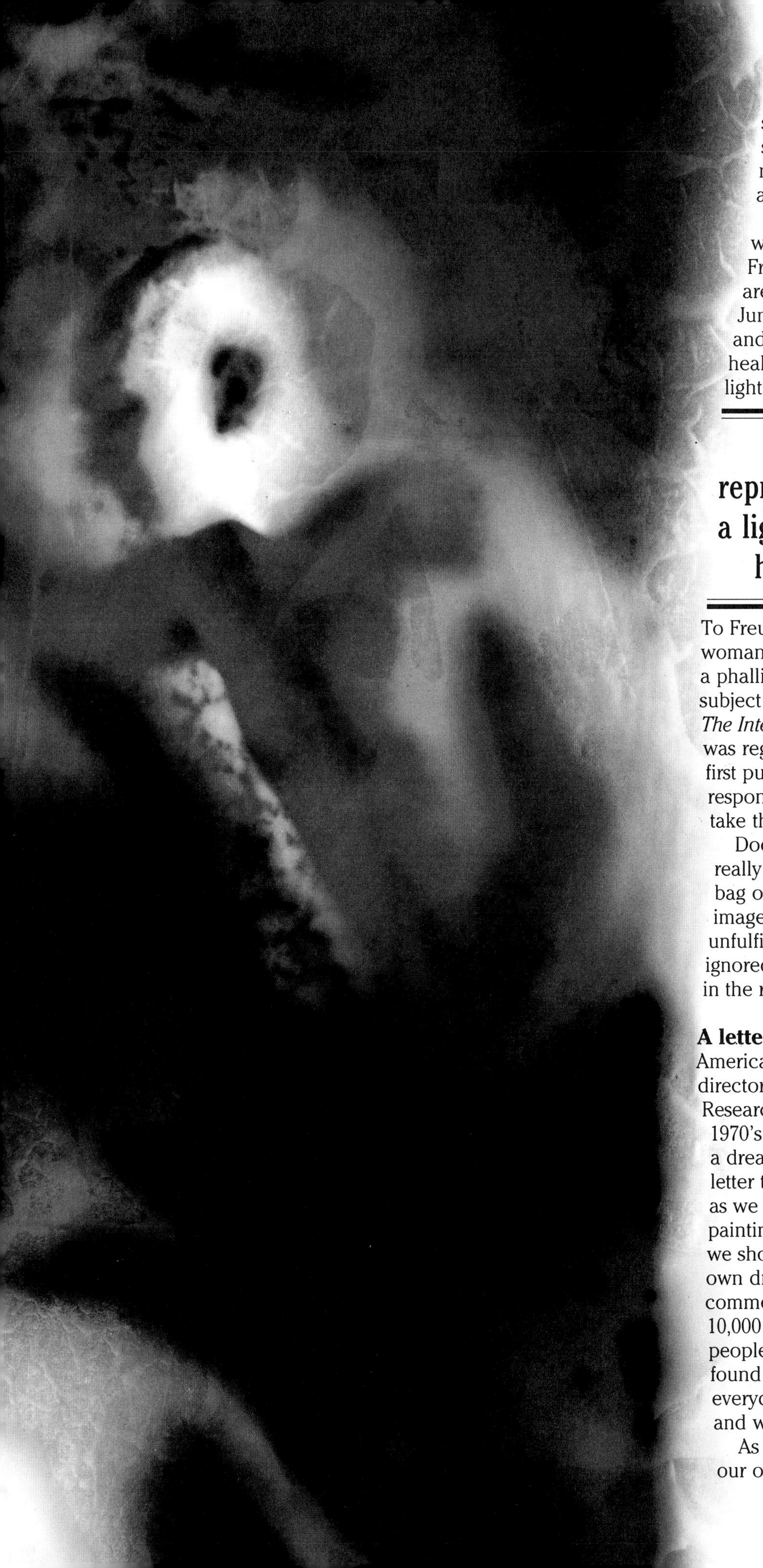

Other images that have widely differing meanings for Freudian and Jungian analysts are houses and lighthouses. To Jung, a house represented the self and a lighthouse indicated a healing influence: the casting of light over a dark and turbulent sea.

To Jung, a house represented the self and a lighthouse indicated a healing influence.

To Freud the house represented woman and a lighthouse was clearly a phallic symbol. Freud's views on the subject are to be found in his book, *The Interpretation of Dreams*, which was regarded as revolutionary when first published in 1899. It was largely responsible for inducing people to take their dreams seriously.

Does the content of our dreams really matter? Are they not just a rag-bag of discarded thoughts and images, of repressed fears and unfulfilled desires, which are best ignored while we get on with living in the real world?

A letter to oneself

American psychologist Calvin Hall, director of the Institute of Dream Research in Miami in the 1960's and 1970's, believes not. He suggests that a dream is "a personal document, a letter to oneself." He argues that, just as we can look at an abstract painting and detect a meaning, so we should be able to analyze our own dreams in the same way. Hall's comments are based on a study of 10,000 dreams recorded by normal people. The majority of these were found to be concerned with everyday situations and problems, and were not difficult to decipher.

As well as giving us insights into our own personalities and desires,

85

Snake god
This detail from a Greek sarcophagus shows a man making offerings to a powerful snake deity.

THE UNCERTAIN SYMBOL

To an early Egyptian, the appearance of a snake in a dream was regarded as lucky, indicating a dispute would be resolved. To the Greeks, however, a snake was regarded as a warning of the presence of enemies or of impending sickness, the degree of which could be determined by the power of the snake. If a Hebrew killed a snake in a dream, it foretold a lost livelihood.

In modern times, the snake was regarded as an obvious phallic symbol by Sigmund Freud, the founder of psychoanalysis. But to Carl Jung, founder of analytical psychology, a snake in a dream symbolized a clash between conscious attitudes and instincts.

Chemical clue

There are times, however, when dream imagery might have nothing to do with repressed sexual feelings or hidden thoughts. An anecdote concerning Friedrich August von Kekulé von Stradonitz, Professor of Chemistry at Ghent, Belgium, illustrates this point well. Kekulé had achieved a major advance in the understanding of the structure of carbon-containing compounds, but in 1865 he was having great difficulty in applying his theories to the structure of benzene, which had only six atoms of hydrogen to six atoms of carbon. One day he dreamed of chains of atoms twisting with a snakelike motion. "But look," he wrote, "What was that? One of the snakes had seized hold of its own tail and the form whirled mockingly before my eyes. As if in a flash of lightning, I awoke." That moment of dream-inspired insight led Kekulé to the theory that in benzene the carbon atoms were joined into a six-sided ring — a discovery that was to revolutionize organic chemistry.

our dreams might even give us a glimpse of our future. One of the best legends of dream prediction concerns John Chapman, a tinker and peddler who lived in 15th-century England. Chapman was told in a dream to go from his home in Swaffham, Norfolk, to London, and to wait on London Bridge. He was so impressed by the dream that he followed the command. It took him three days to walk the hundred miles to the capital. For three more days he waited on the famous bridge but no one spoke to him. As he was about to set off home, a shopkeeper, puzzled by his behavior, came out and asked him what he was waiting for. Chapman told him, but without revealing his name or where he had come from.

Buried treasure

The shopkeeper laughed merrily. "Now if I heeded dreams I might have proved myself as very a fool as thou hast; for it is not long since that I dreamt that at a place called Swaffham Market, in Norfolk, dwells one John Chapman, a peddler. He hath a tree in his back garden, so I dreamed, under which is buried a pot of money. Now suppose I

journeyed all the way thither because of that dream in order to dig for that money, what a fool I should be!" According to this charming but fanciful legend, Chapman returned home immediately and found a vast fortune of gold and silver coins buried under a tree. He used some of the money to help build a church at Swaffham. The story of his dream is commemorated in its stained-glass windows and wood carvings.

Unfinished business

Finding buried treasure apart, are there any benefits in understanding the significance of our dreams? Psychiatry generally takes the view that a dream serves its purpose by giving expression to psychological forces that would be potentially disruptive if left buried in the subconscious. It does not matter, then, whether we can interpret our dreams or even remember them. But Gestalt therapists (who believe that no part of an individual's behavior can be separated from the rest of his or her personality) see dreams as indicating a person's "unfinished business." Psychologists of this school encourage the individual to discover through dramatization the meaning of their experience while asleep.

Because we all dream, it is a subject we can all study personally. On average, we sleep for one-third of our lives, and we dream for many hours during the course of a week. If we live to 75 years of age, we will have spent several years dreaming. The rich tapestry that is revealed to us during that time, if properly understood, might greatly enhance our lives.

Lucky peddler
The strange tale of John Chapman, the Norfolk peddler, is commemorated in his local church and on the signpost of the village where he lived.

INTERPRETING YOUR DREAMS

Some people regard their dreams as amusing and irrelevant fiction. Others are convinced that they are significant. Why not record your dreams, and see if they have a message for you?

THE BEST WAY TO START interpreting your dreams is to keep a special diary by your bed. When you awaken and recall a dream, write it down immediately, noting the date and time. You should also number each dream. Record as much information as you can recall about the experience, including names of people or places, if given, as well as your feelings or mood. Being methodical about dating and numbering dreams is important because this will enable you to check developments and detect recurring themes.

Having done this you can begin to analyze what your dreams are telling you. Much of their content, you will recognize, is inspired by events that have occurred the day before.

Action replay
Your mind may give you an action replay of an encounter with a friend, or you may find yourself with that friend in a situation that is totally different from real life. Do not discard these dreams because you feel your mind has simply mixed up the mental impressions of the preceding day. Look, instead, for a message in the dream drama. Did you notice a difference, however small, in the way the action replay unfolded, compared with the real situation? If so, that difference may be symbolically important, giving you an insight into your own motives and desires, or those of the other people involved.

If your dream showed you in a completely different environment, look for clues as to why this should be. Is your subconscious telling you that you could have handled the encounter better? Or is it trying to draw attention to something your conscious mind may not have detected in the situation? Allow your mind free reign to look for associations, puns, and metaphors. If you are still perplexed by the dream, turn to a book that offers a dictionary of dream signs and symbols. The following are based on such a dictionary in Nerys Dee's *Your Dreams and What They Mean* (Outlook Books, 1985):

Afternoon *can be either a specific time, or may symbolize middle age.*

Bells *can be either a warning sign or a joyous announcement.*

Cat *may symbolize the psychic senses; a black cat can be a metaphor for good fortune.*

Dance *is a symbolic prelude to lovemaking.*

Embroidery *warns you to be careful of gross exaggeration.*

Feathers *are the good things in life.*

Grasshopper *tells you not to jump to conclusions.*

Hair *symbolizes sexual powers.*

Iceberg *is a warning to beware what lies beneath the surface.*

Joseph, dream interpreter
The most famous interpreter of dreams is Joseph, whose story is told in Genesis 41:14 – 36. This 19th-century illustration shows him being summoned from his dungeon by the pharaoh.

Juggler *tells you to rearrange your plans.*

Kiss *is a symbol of being singled out for a special purpose.*

Lace *is a secret love.*

Mansion *represents the whole person: body, mind, and spirit.*

Naked *indicates guilty feelings or the bare truth.*

Orange *means sunshine, cheerfulness, and good health.*

Penguin *gives notice of difficulties ahead.*

Quay *advises you to make the most of the calm before the storm.*

Rice *is an indication of domestic good news.*

Saw *is a warning of being cut down to size.*

Tea *is a sign of innocent friendship, at least at present.*

Umbrella *tells you to take shelter from the storms of life.*

Violin *symbolizes emotional harmony.*

Waiter *means to be of service to others.*

X-ray *suggests that there are unseen forces at work; expect changes.*

Yew tree *advises that there is nothing that can be done to alter facts.*

Zodiac *warns that fame and fortune are in the balance.*

CHAPTER FOUR

The Hand of Fate

*Some methods of divination
are based on chance patterns
usually obtained as a result of
some manual operation. These
are known as aleatory methods.
They include selecting yarrow
stalks, casting divining sticks,
and throwing dice.*

We have all heard the phrase "the luck of
the draw," meaning the chance result of
some random action such as shuffling a
deck of cards or rolling dice. Some people
claim that the results of such random
actions can be used to predict the future,
arguing that, in a sense, chance may be
more than chance, being part of a cosmic
pattern that we can sometimes glimpse
briefly but that we do not fully understand.

The most notable of those who have
made such claims in the present century
was the immensely influential Swiss

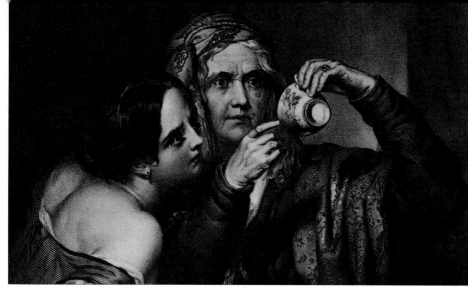

Gypsy fortune teller, c. 1840

READING TEA LEAVES

Telling fortunes from tea leaves, and less commonly from coffee grounds, has been popular since the 19th century. To read the leaves, keep a small quantity of tea in the cup. Swirl the cup clockwise three times and then carefully pour off the liquid. Then turn the teacup upside down. The pattern of the leaves, or grounds, that remains in the bottom of the cup can then be interpreted.

Images and symbols

The leaves, or grounds, will not give precise pictures but suggest images. A bird, an angel, or a bell, for example, means good news; a boat indicates a visit from a friend. Other symbols often found are a gate, meaning change, and clouds, representing trouble.

Sticks of fortune
A North Vietnamese fortune teller prepares to cast divining sticks in order to predict the future.

psychiatrist Carl Gustav Jung (1875–1961). He speculated that: "Everything done at a particular moment of time has the quality of that moment of time." By this Jung meant that many events that seem to be purely coincidental are linked to one another by some greater reality, even though one has not directly caused the other.

This is not a straightforward concept to grasp. We are used to thinking in terms of cause and effect — for example, a ball on a pool table being set into motion when hit by a cue. Some things, however, do happen at the same time without being causally connected. This is what Jung termed "synchronicity" (meaning "time togetherness"). He used this principle to explain the apparent success of fortune tellers.

Meaningful coincidences

An example of time togetherness is somebody who has a 24-hour clock on the wall of his or her kitchen. Each day, when the hands of the clock indicate 1930 hours (7:30 P.M.), that person feels hungry. There is obviously no causal connection between the two events; feeling hungry has not caused the clock to show the time as 1930, nor has the clock showing the time as 1930 caused the feelings of hunger. Yet the events are synchronistically connected to one another — there is a "meaningful

coincidence" between them. The clock showing 1930 and the feeling of hunger both have what Jung called "the quality of that moment of time."

There is evidence that some fortune tellers who have used "random" techniques that rely on the turn of the cards or the fall of the dice have been able to predict the future with greater accuracy than might be expected from chance alone. Yet much of this evidence is anecdotal. Typically somebody says that a fortune teller using some method involving chance has given what proved to be a highly accurate prediction of coming events. In other cases, however, evidence appears to be

Simon Forman

better documented and more solid. The casebooks of Simon Forman (1552–1611), for example, an English astrologer and diviner who lived at the same time as William Shakespeare, survive in the Bodleian Library at Oxford University.

An honest prophet

These casebooks show that as a fortune teller Forman was utterly honest with himself: he recorded details of not only his predictive successes but of his failures, partial or complete. Forman's predictions appear to be far more accurate than might be accounted for by chance. His successes led one distinguished modern English historian, A. L. Rowse, to suggest that he may have had psychic powers. For example, Forman wrote an accurate prediction of the outcome of a particular military expedition to Ireland even before the force had left England.

Irish campaign

The expedition in question was led by the Earl of Essex, a favorite of Queen Elizabeth I, and it was assumed by most people at the English court that it would overcome the Irish rebels without too much difficulty. Yet the entry in Forman's diary for March 19, 1599, recorded that Essex's military adventure would result in "treason, hunger, sickness and death...."

Roman divination
The ancient Romans used to select lines from Virgil's Aeneid *at random as a method of predicting the future.*

imprisoned and eventually beheaded for high treason.

Forman's predictive methods included interpreting either random marks made on sheets of paper, or an astrological chart for the exact moment he was asked a question.

If Forman's predictive techniques were in fact successful, this would be in accord with Jung's theory of synchronicity. It could also be explained in terms of traditional occult theories. There is an ancient idea that the random movements of the diviner's hand when, for instance, he or she throws dice or makes marks upon a sheet of paper, are controlled by the influence of "good spirits" upon the diviner's mind. There is another theory that the diviner has an unconscious prophetic ability, deep within his or her mind, that controls such actions, so that they are not random movements at all.

There is an ancient idea that the supposedly random movements of the diviner's hand are controlled by the influence of "good spirits."

the end will be evil to himself, for he shall be imprisoned....He shall find many enemies on his return and have great loss of goods and honour...."

Beheaded for treason

And just as Forman had predicted, so it happened. Essex left for Ireland in April 1599 and, ignoring his queen's orders, made a disadvantageous truce with the rebels. When he returned to England, Elizabeth stripped him of office and confiscated all his property. His reputation was destroyed. He was

METHODS OF DIVINATION

Various methods are used by fortune tellers as a basis for their interpretations. These include:

◆ Opening a revered book, such as the Bible, at random and taking the first sentence your eye or finger falls on as a text.
◆ Studying the patterns that tea leaves or coffee grounds leave in the bottom of a cup.
◆ Using the random numbers generated by the fall of dice or the flip of coins.
◆ Using the random numbers generated by dividing 49 yarrow stalks into piles (the traditional method for the *I Ching*).
◆ Observing the turn of cards, either conventional, runic, or Tarot decks.
◆ Making rows of holes at random in a box of sand or earth.
◆ Making random marks on a piece of paper.

On the face of it such techniques seem unlikely to predict the future or to give sensible advice to an inquirer. However, millions of people believe in the interpretations that are based on these techniques, and in some cases, they have proved astonishingly accurate.

Palm nut oracle
This carved wooden bowl is used by the priests of the Yoruba people of Nigeria, West Africa, in practicing divination. It contains 16 palm nuts that are cast like dice. The pattern they form determines which verses from a vast collection of oral poetry should be recited in response to a questioner's petition.

THE BOOK OF CHANGES

For 3,000 years people have been consulting the I Ching ***about future events, great and small, in their lives. Fortune tellers claim that, despite its great antiquity, the*** I Ching's ***advice is as relevant today as it ever was.***

HE *I CHING* (meaning "Book of Changes") is the oldest of the world's many books of divination. These, like the oracle at Delphi in ancient Greece, are held to be founts of unearthly wisdom, capable of answering questions about the future. For millennia men and women have used them to find out which course of action they should follow in a particular situation, or how a situation would be resolved.

A book of answers

Few of these oracle books were originally compiled as such — many of them were books so venerated as literature that people began to look upon them almost as actual personalities who might be asked for advice. One of these, for example, was the *Aeneid*, the saga of Aeneas, a refugee from ancient Troy and the legendary founder of Rome. The epic was written by the Latin poet Virgil (70–19 B.C.).

From late classical times until well into the 17th century an inquirer who wished to use the *Aeneid* as an oracle would first write or speak a specific question. Then he or she would open a copy at random and, equally randomly, stab his or her finger on one of the pages. These actions would be repeated twice, and the three lines upon which the finger of the inquirer had fallen would be carefully noted down, and then interpreted to give an answer to the question.

Ancient Chinese oracle

Much older than the *Aeneid*, the basic core of the *I Ching* is one of the few oracle books that was actually compiled for this purpose, at a date probably no later than the 12th century B.C. According to tradition, which may be historically inaccurate, its compilers were King Wen, who ruled a large part of what is now China in about 1150 B.C., and his son, the duke of Chou, a man said to be of great wisdom.

Age-old wisdom
For thousands of years the Chinese have venerated the pronouncements of the I Ching. *At first glance the commentaries appear to have no relevance to the modern reader, but as the symbolism in the verses is contemplated, the timeless wisdom of the* I Ching *may become apparent.*

The sections of the *I Ching* attributed to them were derived from even earlier traditional material dating from a period before any form of writing had developed in China. By the time of Confucius, some 2,500 years ago, the *I Ching* was looked on not just as an oracle book but as a classic work of mystical philosophy. Confucius himself is recorded as having said: "If years were added to my life span I would devote

> ## "If years were added to my life span I would devote them all to the study of the *I Ching*."
> **Confucius**

them all to the study of the *I Ching*." Some commentaries on the book are attributed to Confucius and his disciples, while later ones date from the Ming era, which came to an end in 1644.

When it was first compiled, and the earliest commentaries were written, the *I Ching*'s text was regarded as sacred. It was consulted only by the upper classes who ruled the Celestial Empire of China and by the scholars whom they so respected. As the centuries passed, however, copies of the *I Ching* circulated more widely. Fortune tellers began to use the book to answer the questions of clients from the merchant and peasant classes.

Universal oracle
Until 1949, when the Communists came to power in mainland China, such fortune tellers were found in every Chinese town. They treated both manuscript and printed copies with enormous respect,

◆ PAGE 96   93

CONSULTING THE *I CHING*

The 64 hexagrams of the I Ching *are said to provide illuminating answers to questions asked of the oracle. The appropriate hexagrams are selected by a process traditionally involving yarrow stalks.*

To generate a hexagram begin by formulating a question. How you ask your question is important. The *I Ching* cannot answer such questions as: "Shall I get a promotion?" That depends on the choices an individual makes. The question should be phrased as: "What should I do to get a promotion?" The *I Ching* may indicate the possible ways of proceeding to achieve the desired result.

M

M

M

Casting a hexagram

Having formulated your question, take 50 yarrow stalks. (Any bundle of 50 uniformly long, thin sticks will do.) Before you begin, remove one stalk and put it to one side. By tradition only 49 stalks are actually used. Divide the remaining stalks into two roughly equal piles. Take a single stalk from the right-hand pile and place it between the ring finger and the little finger of your left hand. Remove four stalks at a time from the left-hand pile until four or fewer stalks remain. Put these between the ring and the middle fingers of the left hand.

Repeat this procedure with the right-hand pile, and put the stalks that remain between the first and the middle fingers of the left hand. Place all the stalks that are held in the left hand in a separate pile that is called Heap One. For mathematical reasons there must always be either 5 or 9 sticks in Heap One. If you get a different number, you have made a mistake in counting out the stalks and must start over.

Take all the remaining stalks, except those in Heap One, divide them into two roughly equal piles, and

then repeat the whole procedure. The stalks you have in your left hand now form Heap Two. This pile must always contain either 4 or 8 stalks; any other number indicates a mistake. Repeat the procedure with the remaining stalks to form Heap Three; once again there should be either 4 or 8 stalks. If you end up with another number, you have made an error and the procedure needs to be repeated.

Ritual numbers

Add up the total of stalks in your three heaps. If the process has been correctly carried out, this total will invariably be 25, 21, 17, or l3. These totals convert into what are called "ritual numbers." This is done in accordance with the following rule: if the total number is 25, then the ritual number is 6; if 21, it is 7; if 17, it is 8; if 13, it is 9. If the number converts to a 6 or 8, draw a broken line as the bottom line of your hexagram; if it is 7 or 9, draw a solid line. If the ritual number you end up with is 6 or 9, then mark an *M* beside the line you have drawn.

Once you have formed the first line of the hexagram, the whole procedure is repeated, step by step, a further five times. The first repetition provides the line above the bottom line of your hexagram, and this is continued until your fifth repetition provides you with the top line of your hexagram.

If you have any lines with an *M* marked beside them they are "moving lines," that is, they are in transition from one state to its opposite. Thus a broken line with an *M* beside it is in the process of becoming an unbroken line, and vice versa. When you read the text for the hexagram you have created,

---

Hexagram 29 — Water
"Do not compromise your ideals....If you stick to your guns, following your principles with sincerity and determination, you will attain your goal and overcome the barriers which obstruct your progress."

---

then you must also read the text appropriate to the moving line. Such text always begins with the phrase "six [or nine] in the first [through sixth] place." It must be remembered that when the *I Ching* refers to something as being in "the first place" it means the bottom line of the hexagram; a hexagram is always read from bottom to top. The text relating to the moving lines is very important; if the meaning of a moving line, or lines, contradicts the meaning of the original hexagram, it is the former that is significant.

Paging the oracle

Here is an actual example. Nancy wants to find out if there is a future in her relationship with her boyfriend, Chuck. Her question is: "What are Chuck's feelings for me?" (She does not ask, for example, "Will Chuck fall in love with me?" as the answer to that question depends on an individual exercising his free will.) What the *I Ching* can reportedly do is give an overview of the nature of a situation. The questioner can then determine his or her course of action.

Nancy's totals for the six lines of her hexagram are: 25, 13, 17, 17, 21, and 25, which convert to the ritual numbers 6, 9, 8, 8, 7, and 6. This gives a figure with unbroken lines in the second and fifth places. Nancy consults her copy of the *I Ching*. This figure is Hexagram 29 (left).

Understanding the hexagram

There are a number of different translations of the *I Ching* — Nancy consults Francis X. King's *Encyclopedia of Fortune-telling* (Smith's Publishers, 1988). This gives a paraphrase in modern language of all the hexagrams.

Hexagram 29 is known as "Water." In the *I Ching* water symbolizes danger, which indicates a warning about Nancy's relationship.

The next step is to read the commentary on the moving lines for Hexagram 29. The ritual numbers indicate that there are three moving lines — in the first, second, and sixth lines of the hexagram. The six in the

first line indicates that there is danger all around. This could indicate some mishap in Nancy's relationship. The nine in the second line indicates that if disaster occurs, then Nancy should not despair completely. However, recovery from any such event may be slow. The six in the sixth line indicates that it is best for Nancy to follow the line of least resistance. Nancy needs to look for the easiest way out of danger, and when this is found she should not look back.

The next step is to convert the three moving lines in Hexagram 29 into their opposites. This means that the broken lines in the first and sixth lines become unbroken lines. In the second line the unbroken line becomes broken. This creates a new hexagram that will complete the oracle's answer. The new hexagram is Hexagram 42. Hexagram 29 seemed to indicate that Nancy's relationship with Chuck is fraught with perils. The new hexagram is decisive. Hexagram 42, known as "Increase," indicates that the matter will end well if Nancy is prepared to consider Chuck's needs and to take risks. A modern interpretation of the verse is: "If you are aware of the need to consider others' requirements, you can now successfully engage in bold enterprises."

Hexagram 42 — Increase

"'To rule is to serve' is one of the fundamental axioms....If you are aware of the need to consider others' requirements, you can now successfully engage in bold enterprises and make major changes in your life."

The oracle interpreted

The text of the hexagram and the commentary upon it seem to indicate that Nancy's relationship has all the necessary elements to end well in the course of time, probably as the result of an unexpected stroke of good fortune. However, the negative aspects in Hexagram 29 seem to indicate early difficulties. If the process of generating the hexagrams had been reversed — if the first hexagram had been 42 and the moving lines had transformed it into 29 — the answer would have to be interpreted quite differently. In this case the oracle would be saying that initial good fortune had created a situation in which great danger threatened.

Village fortune teller
The diviner using the I Ching *was a familiar sight in towns and villages throughout Asia. This advertising card, dating from 1904, shows a Korean fortune teller consulting the* I Ching. *The card is one of a series on different methods of fortune telling that was given away with a brand of German meat extract.*

Chinese tiger
In Taoist philosophy the tiger symbolizes the force of yin, which represents the female energy in the universe.

keeping them wrapped in silk when not in use and storing them on a shelf above the shoulder level of a full-grown man.

The fan of fate
Underlying the text of the *I Ching* is a mystical philosophy of great subtlety and power. Its pronouncements on the future tend to avoid the fatalistic approach of many other types of fortune telling. The sages who compiled the *I Ching* believed in human free will; they thought that by responding to events in a manner harmonious with the cosmic order, men and women could make their own destiny. As Taoists they believed that "Fate is fan-shaped." In other words, any choice we make, metaphorically speaking, leads us to a different point on the "fan" that is the future. The advice given to the genuine inquirer is intended not just to forecast the future. It is more personal and helpful than that, since it is designed to enable the inquirer to find his or her way to a desired point in the future.

The *I Ching* is intended to give advice to the "superior man" — which in this context also means the superior woman. The *I Ching* defines the superior man in a very different way from, for example, *The Wall Street Journal*. It values enlightenment above power or material wealth. People considered eminent in our society may even be regarded with contempt by the "personality" of the *I Ching*.

A writer on mystical subjects, Francis X. King, was asked by a well-known architect at a dinner party in 1971 to use the *I Ching* to give the answer to a question he would not disclose. King reluctantly agreed to do this. The answer the *I Ching* provided was: "There is no

---

The sages who compiled the *I Ching* believed in human free will.

---

skin on the thigh; walking is difficult." This answer proved to be true in the most literal sense. The man's question had been about the health of his wife, who had just had skin removed from her thigh for a skin graft to her foot.

The man repeated his question. Once again, he received the same answer. When he asked the question a third time, the *I Ching*'s response was: "At the first question I answer the young fool, but if he asks two or three times I refuse to give an answer."

Those who regularly consult the *I Ching* would not dream of asking the same question of the oracle three times in a row. Instead the questioner would ponder the advice it gave, trying to interpret its meaning within the context of the situation that prompted the inquiry.

A language of symbols
The oracle answers in symbolic language, full of ancient aphorisms. It refers, for example, to the domestic habits of tigers, to the way a young fox walks upon a frozen lake, and to sending armies into battle. Such allusions can seldom be taken literally. They should be interpreted according to the nature of the question.

In a present-day context, for example, a reference to a "proclamation at the court of the King" could refer to a declaration of love, a marriage proposal, a job advertisement, a diagnosis by a doctor, or even a presidential statement. Anyone who starts to consult the *I Ching* will soon learn what is required.

YIN AND YANG

For thousands of years the image of the circle containing the yin and yang symbols has been at the center of Chinese philosophy.

AT THE HEART OF ancient Chinese thought is the idea that all matter is made up of negative and positive energy, and these opposing, yet complementary, forces go to make up the universe. According to ancient Taoist philosophy from which the *I Ching* developed, these forces are symbolized by yin and yang. Yin represents female energy and all that is dark, passive, and absorbing. Yang is associated with masculine energy and everything that is strong and penetrating.

Chinese dragon
The dragon symbolizes yang, the masculine force.

These elements are usually depicted as the dark and light halves of a circle; yin being dark and yang being light. The halves are intertwined, symbolizing how interrelated and interdependent yin and yang are. In the center of each half is a small light or dark seed. It is the combination of the two forces that creates a whole: one is not complete without the other. However, the forces of yin and yang are not regarded as irreconcilable. They are constantly drawn toward each other and for a time they merge and then separate again.

The hexagrams

Every line of the 64 hexagrams that comprise the *I Ching* is either a yin or a yang line. Historians of the *I Ching* believe that when this method of divination was first developed the yin and yang lines were interpreted in a very straightforward fashion: the broken yin line indicated the answer no; the unbroken yang line denoted the answer yes.

Over the centuries this initial simple interpretation became increasingly sophisticated. Chinese sages held that all phenomena and experiences were the result of the interaction between yin and yang.

Protective symbol
This detail from a Chinese door panel shows a classic depiction of yin and yang at the center of a circle. This design was intended to ward off evil spirits at the threshold of the home.

So the hexagrams began to be taken as representing change and flux in the universe. The texts that came to be associated with each of the hexagrams over the centuries described these changes and explained them in a way accessible to the human mind. So, for example, the "soft" yin lines that surround a "hard" yang line in a hexagram could be interpreted as revealing that something that appears soft on the outside may be discovered to be hard and immovable within.

Celestial harmony

The ancient Chinese philosophers saw a universal harmony in the way that night follows day; both are necessary and neither can exist without the other. In their everyday lives, the Chinese sought to create a similar harmony between, for example, the body and mind, and men and women. The wise words of the *I Ching* are one expression of this aspiration.

HEADS OR TAILS?

The traditional way of generating a hexagram is by using a bunch of yarrow stalks. But there are several "shorthand" methods of consulting the I Ching.

ONE QUICK, RELIABLE WAY of arriving at an *I Ching* hexagram is by tossing three coins. While this process is not as ancient as that involving yarrow stalks, it has been used for many hundreds of years and is still favored by Chinese fortune tellers in Taiwan, Singapore, Macao, and Hong Kong. There is no need to go to the expense of buying old Chinese coins for this method — although some people feel that using such coins adds atmospheric punch to their divinations. Nickels, dimes, or quarters serve the purpose just as well.

Shorthand hexagrams

The method is quite straightforward. Start by deciding that one side of each of your three coins will have a value of 2, and the other side a value of 3. It is important to be consistent, sticking to the number/side equivalents you have chosen. Toss all the coins together and add up the totals of the sides showing. This total *has* to be 6, 7, 8, or 9. If you get a different number, you have made a mistake in your computing, and need to count up the values of the coins again.

Write down your total and then throw the coins again, putting the second total *above* the first. Repeat this procedure a further four times, putting each successive total *above* the previous ones. In this way the top figure of the six totals will be the one you threw last. By each of the totals that is an even number draw a broken line; by each odd number draw an unbroken line. By each 6 and 9 write an *M*. For example, if your successive throws were 8, 8, 7, 9, 8, and 8 you would note down your hexagram as shown below.

M

Hexagram 62 — Triumph of the small

As with a hexagram created by the traditional yarrow stalk method, any line with an *M* beside it indicates a "moving line." Such a line is in the process of turning, or moving, into its opposite. So a broken line is moving toward becoming an unbroken line, and an unbroken line is moving toward becoming a broken line. The hexagram you have created from the fall of the coins is Hexagram 62. Changing the moving line into its opposite, Hexagram 62 turns into Hexagram 15, which is shown below.

Hexagram 15 — Modesty

When interpreting the answer indicated by the throw of the coins, follow the same sequence as if you had created a hexagram using the yarrow stalks method: first read the commentary on Hexagram 62; next read the relevant text for any moving lines in this hexagram. (It is important to remember that when the *I Ching* refers to the "first place" this means the bottom line of your hexagram, and "the last place" means the top line.) Finally, to complete your reading, turn to the text for Hexagram 15.

The six-wand method

Another simple and quick way to create a hexagram is by casting six sticks, or wands. Originally these wands were made out of ivory, tortoiseshell, or precious woods. Today special sets of wands can be purchased at stores that offer Chinese goods. They are eight inches

One quick, reliable way of arriving at an *I Ching* hexagram is by tossing three coins.

long and about one inch wide, and approximately one-eighth of an inch thick. They are painted black on both sides with a band of white painted across the middle of one side. If you have difficulty in obtaining these wands, popsicle sticks that are painted appropriately do just as well.

To create the hexagram, shuffle the wands while at the same time concentrating on the question you want to ask the oracle. When you feel ready to stop shuffling, allow the wands to roll from your hand onto a flat surface, as if you were unrolling a small mat. The wand that falls nearest to you forms the first, or bottom, line of your hexagram. When a wand falls with the black side uppermost, this indicates that you draw an

Some versions of the *I Ching* remain faithful to the original, translating literally each of the 64 hexagrams. At first, because of the old-fashioned and heavily symbolic language, these editions may not seem accessible to the modern-day reader. Yet with careful reading the relevance of the words may become apparent.

The two most widely used translations in this category are: *The I Ching* (Dover Books, 1986) translated by James Legge in 1889, and Richard Wilhem's 1924 edition, *The I Ching* (Princeton University Press, 1961) which also includes a foreword by Jung.

Modern reworkings

Many modern editions of the *I Ching* are widely available. In these versions the commentaries have been reworked to make them more accessible to the modern-day reader. We have used Francis X. King's version from *The Encyclopedia of Fortune-telling* (Smith's Publishers, 1988).

> The six-wand method of creating a hexagram is a good way to start familiarizing yourself with the *I Ching*.

Divination by dice
This page of a 16th-century manuscript by Maistre Laurens l'Esprit demonstrates how to find out if a wife can produce sons.

unbroken line. If the white band is uppermost, this indicates that you draw a broken line. Once you have drawn out the broken and unbroken lines that go to make up your hexagram, you can look up the appropriate text.

The six-wand method of creating a hexagram is a good way to start familiarizing yourself with the *I Ching*. But this method does not give the fullest possible reading, because the fall of the wands does not take into account the influence of any moving lines that may occur when yarrow stalks are used to create a hexagram.

Roll of the dice

The simple roll of a pair of dice can also be used to form a hexagram. Throw the dice and total the dots, disregarding all throws that do not total 6, 7, 8, or 9. The use of dice is not traditionally Chinese. However, they have been used in Western fortune telling since classical

times, and so their use may be looked upon as being hallowed by antiquity.

Predictive techniques

The use of dice in divination is not restricted solely to the *I Ching*. There are many other predictive techniques that can be worked out using the roll of the dice. The method given below is used for questions that can be answered by a simple yes or no.

◆ Draw a circle about seven inches in diameter.
◆ Formulate your question and throw three dice into the circle.
◆ Total them, disregarding any dice that have fallen outside the circle.
◆ The totals can be interpreted in the following way:

0 Ask again in a week.
1 Yes.
2 Ask again in three weeks.
3 Ask again in a lunar month — exactly four weeks from today.
4 Yes, if you aren't too selfish.
5 No, unless you are more careful than usual.
6 Yes, stop worrying.
7 Yes, if you employ your strength and self-reliance.
8 Yes, if you work along with others.
9 Yes, but only if you persist and work at things.
10 No, unless you stop worrying.
11 The matter is too uncertain to be sure.
12 Only if you are serious about things.
13 Yes, if you are prudent and skeptical.
14 Yes, most certainly.
15 Yes, if you behave very decisively and make sure of what is going on.
16 No, unless you are true to your inner nature.
17 No, unless you are prepared to take risks.
18 No at the moment — but maybe yes at some time in the future.

CASTING THE RUNES

An alternative form of fortune telling has enjoyed a resurgence of popularity in recent years. It is based on the magical letters of the ancient Nordic alphabets.

RUNES ARE THE LETTERS of ancient Nordic alphabets, which had varying numbers of letters, ranging from 16 to 31. The one usually used by contemporary fortune tellers contains 24 letters.

The letters of the runic alphabets were associated with magic and the supernatural from a very early date. The very word *rune* was derived from a root word that meant "mysterious, hidden." There is an ancient Norse poem that includes a passage that reads: "A twelfth magic I know...I cut and paint runes...the [dead] man walks and talks with me."

Those who tell fortunes by casting the runes reportedly achieve impressive results. The runic letters are said to correlate with archetypal and other powerful forces in the human collective unconscious. No method of divination using runes is altogether traditional. This is because no one, not even the anthropologists and ancient historians, is sure exactly how the ancient Nordic priesthood divined by means of runes.

Magicians and runesticks
This 17th-century illustration is from A Compendious History of the Goths, Swedes and Vandals. *It shows Scandinavian magicians casting runes. The runic characters can be clearly seen on their runesticks, but no one knows what technique they used to make their prophecies.*

A deck of runes

Here is a very simple method of "casting the runes." Inscribe each of the 24 rune letters shown here on to a card. Concentrate on what your attitude should be in relation to a situation that concerns you; then shuffle and cut the pack to reveal a card. Interpret the rune letter on the card you have cut according to this chart.

ᛒ *FEOH Success and happiness*	ᛜ *YER Be patient*
ᚫ *UR Good fortune if no risks are taken*	ᛄ *YR Stay calm*
ᚦ *THORN Take no risks*	ᛢ *PEORTH Take no chances and you may be lucky*
ᚨ *AS Be wary*	ᛉ *AKZI Be decisive*
ᚱ *RIT Be prudently adventurous*	ᛋ *SIG Relax; be calm*
ᚲ *KAON Grasp available opportunities*	ᛏ *TIW Take action*
ᚷ *GIFU Take others' advice*	ᛒ *BIRCA Take the long-term view*
ᚹ *WUNNA Be grateful for what you already have*	ᛖ *EOH Be very prudent*
ᚻ *HAGAL Events are beyond your control*	ᛗ *MAN Avoid stress*
ᚾ *NAWT Problems ahead*	ᛚ *LAGU Things are not what they seem*
ᛁ *IS No hasty actions*	ᛝ *ING Be flexible*
	ᛟ *ODAL Be patient, unselfish, and active*
	ᛞ *DAG Make haste slowly*

Swedish runes
This runestone, found near Gothenburg in Sweden, dates from the ninth century. Many such runestones are to be found scattered through the Swedish countryside. In Swedish culture runes were used as talismans. They were used to protect, heal, control the weather, and even to help a prisoner escape from his captors. Warriors would often have the runic letters incised on the blades of their swords in order to protect them in battle.

GEOMANCY

Can holes in a box of sand help to forecast your future? Wise men and mystics from several different ancient cultures were convinced that they could.

Tribal wisdom
The tracks of the desert fox are interpreted by the wise men of the Dogon tribe as having a bearing on certain aspects of tribal life.

FOX PRINTS
The Dogon tribe of Mali, West Africa, uses a geomantic method to divine the answers to specific questions, often on the subjects of agriculture or fertility. Before nightfall the seers of the tribe mark out in the sandy ground a grid with symbolic markings relating to the question they want to ask.

Tempting nuts
Peanuts are then scattered over the grid in the sand and left overnight. During the night the peanuts are consumed by desert foxes which leave marks on the grid. In the morning the wise men of the tribe come forward and interpret these markings in relation to the specific question that was asked.

G EOMANCY, WHICH LITERALLY means "fortune telling by means of earth," is derived from the mystical practices of a number of different cultures, including the Chinese, Arab, and non-Arab African. The practice of geomancy spread to Europe in the Middle Ages and was introduced into North America by students of the occult teachings of such 16th- and 17th-century mystics as Cornelius Agrippa (1486–1535) and Robert Fludd (1574–1637).

Four-line figures
While the *I Ching* is concerned with hexagrams, geomancy is concerned with "quadrigrams," that is, four-line figures in which an odd number (called a "zero line") is usually represented by a single cross or asterisk (x or *). When an even number is generated (called a "one line") it is represented by two crosses or asterisks (xx or **). Since there are only four lines in a geomantic figure, there are only 16 possible combinations, as distinct from the 64 possible combinations that go to make up the hexagrams of the *I Ching*.

Sixteen random numbers
One popular method of divining by means of geomancy involves making 16 rows of dots in a box of earth or dry sand in order to generate 16 random numbers, odd or even. A less complicated method of achieving the same result, and one that we know was used by such 16th- and 17th-century diviners as Simon Forman and Robert Fludd, is to make similar marks on a piece of paper.

A simple method of divining is to throw a die or dice four times and note down whether the results are odd or even. If you want to experiment with this method,

A simple method of divining is to throw a die or dice four times and note down whether the results are odd or even.

Wise men from the east
This illustration from the 14th-century manuscript The Travels of Sir John Mandeville *shows Arab geomancers and astrologers.*

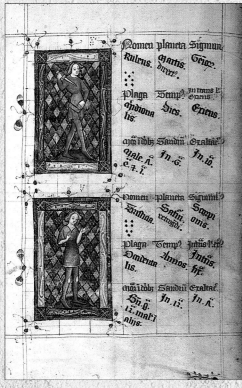

Royal divination
These geomantic and astrological forecasts were compiled in 1391 for the English king Richard II.

begin by formulating your question, writing it down on a piece of paper. As when formulating a query for the *I Ching*, avoid questions of the "either/or" variety. Try to make your question one of the following two sorts: "What will happen if I or so-and-so follows such-and-such a course of action in relation to the situation I am inquiring about?" Alternately you could ask: "How will the situation I am inquiring about resolve itself for me or for the person on whose behalf I am inquiring?"

Try to phrase the question so precisely that you are not misled by the answer you receive; geomancy has a reputation for giving answers to vague divinatory questions that are accurate but extremely misleading. For example, if you are thinking of engaging in a legal action you should not vaguely ask: "Will this legal action be highly profitable?" The answer you get may be a very

decided affirmative — which you may think applies to you but actually means: "Yes, for the other side," or "Yes, for all the attorneys involved in it." In this case, your question should be: "Will legal action prove highly profitable for me?"

Dice divination

Having formulated your question, throw your die or dice four times, noting down with each throw whether the result is an odd or an even number. Mark down two crosses (or asterisks) for each even number you have thrown and a single cross or asterisk for each odd number. If, say, the numbers were, in order of them being thrown, odd, odd, even, even, you would note them down, starting from the top, as shown in Fig. A. If the numbers were even, even, even, odd, you would note them down as in Fig. B.

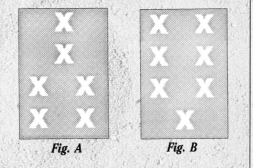

Fig. A   *Fig. B*

The result of throwing your die will be one of the 16 geomantic figures. Now count up the total number of crosses (or asterisks) in the figure you have drawn.

If the total is an odd number, such as in Fig. B (which has a total of seven), this indicates that the matter about which you are asking is in an indeterminate state. This means that the question you have asked cannot be answered at the moment. In this case you must ask again 24 hours later, and continue to ask, if you have to, each successive day until you get a figure containing an even number of crosses. This will be one of eight figures whose divinatory significance can be interpreted in accordance with the "Geomantic Figures" key on the right.

GEOMANTIC FIGURES

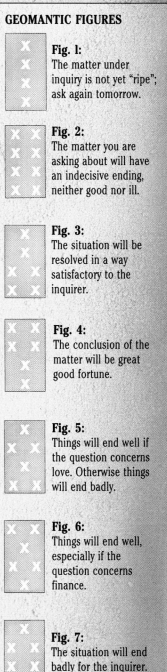

Fig. 1:
The matter under inquiry is not yet "ripe"; ask again tomorrow.

Fig. 2:
The matter you are asking about will have an indecisive ending, neither good nor ill.

Fig. 3:
The situation will be resolved in a way satisfactory to the inquirer.

Fig. 4:
The conclusion of the matter will be great good fortune.

Fig. 5:
Things will end well if the question concerns love. Otherwise things will end badly.

Fig. 6:
Things will end well, especially if the question concerns finance.

Fig. 7:
The situation will end badly for the inquirer.

Fig. 8:
An unsatisfactory conclusion for the inquirer, neither very good nor bad.

CHAPTER FIVE

PAPER PROPHETS

Cartomancy, or the use of cards for divination, dates back many centuries. Nowadays the Tarot pack is the one usually employed for this purpose. Cartomancers believe that its mysterious images have a powerful effect on the subconscious mind.

In 1377 Brother Johannes von Rheinfelden, of the Brefeld monastery in Switzerland, wrote that "a certain game called the game of cards has come to us...in which game the state of the world as it is now is most excellently described and figured. But at what time it was invented, where, and by whom, I am entirely ignorant."

This is the first definite mention of playing cards in Europe, although the Chinese probably had them by the 10th century. Brother Johannes's statement suggests that the cards' primary function was to create a

THE MAJOR ARCANA

These Tarot cards are generally numbered and titled as follows:

0	The Fool
I	The Magician/The Juggler
II	The High Priestess/The Popess/Juno
III	The Empress
IIII	The Emperor
V	The Hierophant/The Pope/Jupiter
VI	The Lover(s)
VII	The Chariot
VIII	Justice (transposed with Force/Strength/ Fortitude in some modern packs)
VIIII	The Hermit
X	The Wheel of Fortune
XI	Force/Strength/Fortitude (or Justice – see VIII)
XII	The Hanged Man
XIII	Death
XIIII	Temperance
XV	The Devil
XVI	The Tower (of Destruction)
XVII	The Star
XVIII	The Moon
XVIIII	The Sun
XX	Judg(e)ment/The Angel
XXI	The World/The Universe

The Marseilles Tarot
The French pack that includes these three cards dates from the 17th century. The designs of the Marseilles Tarot had become standardized by the 18th century. It remains the most traditional of the decks in popular use today.

game, but that they also had an instructive purpose. Some experts believe the allegorical images on the cards were designed to teach the principles of society and the cosmos during the Renaissance. Others claim the cards are actually the teachings, in code, of secret cults or societies of the Middle Ages. And some of the images on the cards represent characters who were also featured in carnivals or triumphal parades, chivalric tales, and dramas.

Allegorical scenes

In the 15th century, playing cards became popular throughout Europe. There were a number of local variations, but the basic Tarot pack was slowly standardized, based on the Italian version popular in Venice. In the early 16th century the Marseilles Tarot grew from these roots. It had a total of 78 cards, divided into two different types: the Major Arcana, of which there were 22, and the Minor Arcana, of which there were 56. The Major Arcana (also known as Greater Arcana), depict allegorical scenes with full-length figures that are generally numbered and titled.

Four suits

The 56 Minor Arcana (also called the Lesser Arcana) are divided into four suits: swords, wands (batons), cups (chalices), and pentacles (coins). Each suit contains 14 cards comprising four court cards – king, queen, male knight (cavalier), and male page (valet) – plus 10 pip or numbered cards, X to I (ace).

The Etteilla Tarot
This enigmatic deck of Tarot cards was designed by a Frenchman named Alliette at the end of the 18th century. It was based on the researches of Antoine Court de Gébelin. References to symbols associated with ancient Egypt (such as the serpents, and the pyramids in the design of the Death card) added a trace of exotic mysticism to the deck.

The suits of the Tarot pack are thought to represent the four divisions of the populace in medieval Europe: swords for soldiers, nobility, and aristocracy; wands for peasants, workers, and the lower classes; cups for the clergy and ecclesiastical groups; and pentacles for tradesmen and the commercial class.

The ordinary deck of 52 cards plus jokers we use today descends from the Tarot pack. The court cards of knight and page in the Tarot combine to form the jack, and The Fool from the Major Arcana resurfaces as the joker. The suits of ordinary playing cards also evolved from those of the Tarot: swords changed to spades,

wands became clubs, cups changed to hearts, pentacles became diamonds.

The earliest printed reference to the use of Tarot cards for divinatory purposes appears in a set of five sonnets on the Major Arcana written by Teofilo Folengo under the pseudonym Merlini Cocai, and included in his verse drama published in Venice in 1527 under the title *Caos del Triperuno*. In the sonnets several noble persons have their fortunes revealed by the Major Arcana.

A popular method of divination

It was not until the late 18th century, however, that divination with Tarot cards became widespread. In *Le Monde Primitif* (1781) the French scholar Antoine Court de Gébelin advanced his theory that the 22 Major Arcana constituted the knowledge contained in the Egyptian hieroglyphic *Book of Thoth*, which he claimed had been saved from the ruins of burning Egyptian temples thousands of years earlier. His theories were adopted and elaborated by Etteilla, a French wigmaker whose real name was Alliette (Etteilla reversed), who produced his own deck of 78 cards.

In the 19th century the use of the Tarot pack as a device for fortune telling became very popular. The French occultist Eliphas Lévi related the designs of the Major Arcana to the 22 letters of the Hebrew alphabet. Thereafter a number of occultists, including S. L. MacGregor Mathers, A. E. Waite, and Aleister Crowley, produced alternative packs with variations dictated by their own mystic theories.

> A number of occultists produced alternative Tarot packs with variations dictated by their own mystic theories.

Tarocchi *players*
This fresco in the Palazzo Poggi in Bologna is by the 16th-century Italian painter Niccolò dell'Abate. The well-dressed young players in the picture are using the card game as an opportunity for amorous flirtation.

THE ORIGINS OF THE TAROT

Tarot cards were not originally used for fortune telling. They were adopted for *tarocchi*, a card game played by Italian nobility that is similar to modern whist or bridge, except that a fifth suit in Tarot acts as trumps and beats cards in the other suits.

Several 15th-century Italian frescoes depict card-players. A fresco dated to the end of the 15th century at the Issogne Castle in Valle d'Aosta shows two men and a woman playing cards. Another fresco at the Casa Borromeo, Milan, shows five young people seated outdoors playing *tarocchi*.

Known as *tarocchi* in Italy, *tarot* in France, and *Tarock* in Germany, the game remained popular for nearly three centuries, until the early 1800's. There were regional variations in the rules, and the decks differed too, but the game was basically the same.

Tarock is still played in Austria, Switzerland, parts of southwestern Germany, and some eastern European countries. Early *Tarock* trumps were often highly artistic and depicted animals, either single-ended or reversible (double-ended), or full-length figures and scenes, including operas, dancers, costumes, weddings, proverbs, mythology, folklore, buildings, cities, and military and historical people and events. *Tarock* packs usually comprise 54 cards, although sometimes they contain 78.

Ancient card game

Another game, similar to *tarocchi*, called *minchiate*, originated in Florence in the 16th century. A pack containing 40 trump cards was specially devised for the game. The trumps were superior to the 56 cards in the other four suits, and with one Fool, the pack totaled 97 cards. The origin of the term *minchiate* is not known for certain, but it may derive from the old Italian word *menchia*, meaning game or sport.

EARLY TAROT CARDS

The earliest Tarot cards were individually made and painted by master craftsmen for the Italian nobility. They are objets d'art of great beauty, and the few surviving cards are very valuable.

ONLY 271 HAND-PAINTED ITALIAN Tarot cards of the 15th century exist today, remnants of some 15 different incomplete packs. These surviving 15th-century cards are oversized, measuring approximately 6 ²/₃ inches high by 3 ¹/₂ inches wide, and are illuminated, with gold-tooled backgrounds.

The heraldic devices of the Visconti and Sforza ducal families of Milan are found on the costumes of many of the figures. It is believed that Bonifacio Bembo, one of the favored court artists of several Sforza dukes, painted many of these cards. Although the cards are unsigned, other works by Bembo are similar in style and imagery.

By the 16th century the use of Tarot cards had spread to France, and many of the 17th- and 18th-century decks were produced there.

Death

Noblet Tarot
The earliest Tarot cards showed Death as a skeleton on horseback. In the 17th century he began to be depicted on foot. This is a 17th-century design by French cardmaker Jean Noblet.

Justice

The Hanged Man

The World

Parisian Tarot
This design is by an unknown 17th-century Parisian cardmaker. At approximately 4 x 1 ³/₄ inches, these cards are smaller and narrower than earlier designs.

The Magician

Gringonneur Tarot
In 1388 Louis of Valois, the duke of Orléans and Touraine, married the daughter of the duke of Milan. She may have been responsible for introducing the Italian pastime of cards to the French royal court. In 1391 the treasurer of the French king, Charles VI, paid Jacquemin Gringonneur to create three packs of gilded cards. If the 17 cards that remain in existence today are genuine, they are the oldest Tarot cards in the world. But some authorities suggest that they may be of 15th-century Venetian origin.

Three of Staves

The Star

Visconti-Sforza Tarot

The largest deck of cards surviving from the 15th century is known as the Visconti-Sforza Tarot. Of the original 78 cards, 74 are still in existence, spread among three collections (two in Bergamo, Italy, and one in New York). The World and The Star (shown here) are two of the six trumps not attributed to Bonifacio Bembo. They were probably painted at a later date by another court artist, Antonio Cicognara, possibly as replacements for lost cards.

Brera Tarot

Another 15th-century Tarot deck can be found in the Brera Gallery in Milan, Italy. There are 48 surviving cards, and they measure approximately 7 x 3 $\frac{1}{2}$ inches. The trump cards of this deck are also attributed to Bonifacio Bembo.

The Fool

Knight of Cups

Queen of Staves

Jerger Tarot

This deck of Tarot cards was woodblock printed and stencil colored by Jean Jerger at Besançon, France, in about 1800. In this deck The Popess and The Pope were replaced by Juno and Jupiter, respectively. At certain periods of history the Catholic Church went through phases when it disapproved of the Tarot, and this change was probably intended to placate the Church.

LE FOU

Modern Tarot Cards

During the 18th and 19th centuries, Tarot cards became increasingly popular in Europe. Woodblock printed cards gave way to lithographed cards, with beautiful images in many colors.

By the 18th century the Tarot deck had become standardized. It consisted of 78 cards, 22 Major Arcana plus 56 Minor Arcana. The Marseilles Tarot, with its crudely drawn and brightly colored full-length figures, was one of the most popular styles.

Today, hundreds of different packs are available. The Native American and Medicine Woman Tarot draw on native American folklore. The Arthurian Tarot, Norse Tarot, and Celtic Tarot packs combine mythological stories with standard Tarot imagery. The Herbal Tarot, Art Nouveau Tarot, and Universal Waite Tarot are among the most popular decks.

The Hero

Persian Tarot
This lithographed card shows a man on horseback fighting a lion. It is from a deck of Persian playing cards in the Tarot tradition published in the 19th century.

Bacchus

Six of Coins

French Revolutionary Tarot
This divinatory deck is related to the Tarot and dates from the late 1790's. It celebrates the ideals and achievements of the French Revolution.

Press Freedom — Light

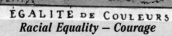

Racial Equality — Courage

Le'Spagnol Capitano Eracasse

Vandenborre Tarot
These Swiss cards are from 18th-century Flemish designs by François-Jean Vandenborre of Brussels. Flemish decks of this period replaced The Popess with the *Le'Spagnol Capitano Eracasse* — a comic figure whose main characteristic was overweening conceit — and The Pope was replaced by Bacchus, the irreverent god of wine and ecstasy.

Florence Tarot
This card is from a *tarocchi* deck published in Florence, Italy, at the end of the 19th century. The cards are based on the designs of the Alessandro Vassone Tarot published in Turin in about 1890. All the Major Arcana and court cards are double-ended, and titled in Italian. The Major Arcana cards have Arabic numerals, including *Il Matto* (The Fool), which in other decks was normally unnumbered.

The Tower

Pamela Colman Smith

RIDER-WAITE TAROT
This deck was issued by William Rider & Son, London, in December 1909. It was designed by an American woman, Pamela Colman Smith, a member of an occult organization called the Order of the Golden Dawn.

She was directed in her work by Arthur Edward Waite, one of the leaders of the Order. He had studied the Tarot and believed that some changes were necessary to bring it closer to its origins.

Russian Tarot
These Russian cards are from a divinatory deck used in a similar way to the Tarot. They date from the early years of the 20th century.

Multilingual Tarot
This card is from a divinatory Tarot pack inspired by Mlle. Le Normand and used in Central Europe in about 1900. The four languages on the card are Hungarian, German, Serbo-Croatian, and Russian.

The Sun

The Key

Multilingual card — The Pope

A new order
The Rider-Waite deck is the first popular pack to depict full scenes and images on the ten numbered cards of the four suits. Waite also transposed two Major Arcana cards, VIII Justice and XI Strength, renumbering them VIII Strength and XI Justice. Waite believed Justice was originally associated with *lamed*, the 12th letter of the Hebrew alphabet. In the Rider-Waite Tarot deck, counting 0 The Fool as the first card and I The Magician as the second, and so on, Justice falls as the 12th card.

The Hermit

Three of Swords

Wealth

PRACTICAL TAROT

This section is designed to familiarize you with one particular deck of cards, the Marseilles Tarot, and to show you how to lay out the cards and make your own readings.

THE TAROT IMAGES used in different decks are basically similar, but there are variations. In this section we are using the earliest standardized deck, the Marseilles Tarot. For each of the cards of the Major Arcana, the ordinary divinatory significance is given first; then the reverse meanings that apply when the card appears to the diviner upside down.

Users of Tarot cards should harness their intuition to interpret the meanings of each card beyond these brief guidelines. For a fuller interpretation, and for the meanings of the 56 Minor Arcana, the reader should consult a reference volume on the Tarot.

**LE MAT
THE FOOL**

**L'IMPÉRATRICE
THE EMPRESS**

**LE BATELEUR
THE MAGICIAN**

**LA PAPESSE
THE HIGH PRIESTESS**

**L'EMPEREUR
THE EMPEROR**

The Fool
DIVINATORY MEANINGS: Beginning of an adventure. Enthusiasm. Initiative. New opportunities beckon. Unlimited possibilities. Folly. Extravagance. REVERSE MEANINGS: Faulty choice or a bad decision. Indecision. Apathy. Hesitation.

I The Magician
DIVINATORY MEANINGS: Originality. Creativity. Free will. Self-reliance. Spontaneity. Self-confidence. Ingenuity. Flexibility. REVERSE MEANINGS: Weakness of will. Ineptitude. Insecurity. Disquiet. Delay.

II The High Priestess
DIVINATORY MEANINGS: Wisdom. Sound judgment. Serene knowledge. Common sense. Learning. Serenity. Objectivity. Perception. Platonic relationships. REVERSE MEANINGS: Ignorance. Shortsightedness. Lack of understanding. Selfishness.

III The Empress
DIVINATORY MEANINGS: Feminine progress. Action. Natural energy. Development. Fruitfulness. Fertility. Mother. Sister. Wife. Marriage. Children. REVERSE MEANINGS: Vacillation. Inaction. Lack of interest. Lack of concentration. Indecision.

IIII The Emperor
DIVINATORY MEANINGS: Worldly power. Accomplishment. Confidence. Wealth. Stability. Authority. Leadership. Father. Brother. Husband. Male dominance. REVERSE MEANINGS: Immaturity. Ineffectiveness. Lack of strength. Indecision. Inability to progress.

LE PAPE
THE POPE

LE CHARIOT
THE CHARIOT

L'HERMITE
THE HERMIT

V The Pope
DIVINATORY MEANINGS:
Ritualism. Ceremonies. Mercy.
Humility. Kindness. Goodness.
Forgiveness. Timidity.
Spiritual leader.
REVERSE MEANINGS: Foolish
exercise of generosity. Excess
of kindness. Repeated errors.
Susceptibility.

VII The Chariot
DIVINATORY MEANINGS:
Fortitude. Perseverance. Major
effort. Voyage or journey.
Escape. Rushing to a decision.
Possible turmoil.
REVERSE MEANINGS: Defeat.
Failure.

VIIII The Hermit
DIVINATORY MEANINGS:
Counsel. Knowledge.
Solicitude. Inner strength.
Self-illumination. Caution.
Vigilance. Withdrawal.
Annulment.
REVERSE MEANINGS:
Imprudence. Hastiness.
Rashness. Prematurity.
Foolish acts.

L'AMOUREUX
THE LOVER

LA JUSTICE
JUSTICE

LA ROUE DE FORTUNE
THE WHEEL OF FORTUNE

VI The Lover
DIVINATORY MEANINGS: Love.
Beauty. Perfection. Harmony.
Unanimity. Trials overcome.
Beginning of a romance.
Emotional involvement.
REVERSE MEANINGS: Failure to
rise to the test. Unreliability.
Separation. Frustration.

VIII Justice
DIVINATORY MEANINGS:
Strength. Control. Courage.
Conviction. Defiance. Action.
Confidence. Accomplishment.
REVERSE MEANINGS: Weakness.
Pettiness. Sickness. Lack of faith.
 (In some modern packs, this
card is transposed with XI
Force/Strength/Fortitude.)

X The Wheel of Fortune
DIVINATORY MEANINGS:
Destiny. Fortune. Fate.
Outcome. Culmination.
Approaching the end of a
problem. Inevitability.
Advancement for better
or worse.
REVERSE MEANINGS: Failure.
Ill luck. Broken sequence.
Unexpected bad fate.

113

XI Force
DIVINATORY MEANINGS: Justice. Fairness. Reasonableness. Harmony. Righteousness. Virtue. Honor. Virginity. Just reward.
REVERSE MEANINGS: Bias. False accusations. Bigotry. Severity. Intolerance. Unfairness.
   (In some modern packs, this card is transposed with VIII Justice.)

XIII Death
DIVINATORY MEANINGS: Transformation. Change. Loss. Failure. Alteration. Clearing away of the old for the new. Ending of a relationship.
REVERSE MEANINGS: Stagnation. Immobility. Slow changes. Partial change. Inertia.

XV The Devil
DIVINATORY MEANINGS: Subordination. Ravage. Bondage. Malevolence. Subservience. Downfall. Lack of success. Weird experience. Bad outside influence.
REVERSE MEANINGS: Release from bondage. Respite. Divorce. Throwing off shackles.

XII The Hanged Man
DIVINATORY MEANINGS: Life in suspension. Transition. Change. Sacrifice. Repentance. Readjustment. Apathy and dullness. Abandonment. Renunciation.
REVERSE MEANINGS: Lack of sacrifice. Unwillingness to exert effort. Failure to commit self.

XIIII Temperance
DIVINATORY MEANINGS: Temperance. Moderation. Patience. Accommodation. Harmony. Mixing together to bring into perfect union. Adjustment. Good influence.
REVERSE MEANINGS: Discord. Conflict of interest. Hostility.

XVI The Tower of Destruction
DIVINATORY MEANINGS: Sudden change. Breakdown of old beliefs. Severing of past relationships. Changing an opinion.
REVERSE MEANINGS: Continued oppression. Following old ways. Living in a rut.

XVII The Star
DIVINATORY MEANINGS: Hope. Faith. Inspiration. Bright prospects. Mixing of the past and present. Optimism. Good omen. Spiritual love. Fulfillment.
REVERSE MEANINGS: Unfulfilled hopes. Disappointment. Pessimism. Bad luck. Lack of opportunity.

XX Judgement
DIVINATORY MEANINGS: Judgment. Atonement. The need to repent and forgive. Rejuvenation. Rebirth. Improvement. Promotion. Favorable developments.
REVERSE MEANINGS: Delay. Disappointment. Failure to face facts. Divorce. Theft.

XVIII The Moon
DIVINATORY MEANINGS: Deception. Obscurity. Trickery. Dishonesty. Disillusionment. Danger. Bad influence. Ulterior motives. False friends.
REVERSE MEANINGS: Deception recognized before damage is done. Trifling mistakes. Overcoming bad temptations.

XVIIII The Sun
DIVINATORY MEANINGS: Satisfaction. Accomplishment. Contentment. Success. Favorable social relationships. Love. Joy. Engagement. Happy marriage.
REVERSE MEANINGS: Unhappiness. Loneliness. Possibly a broken engagement or marriage. Canceled plans.

XXI The World
DIVINATORY MEANINGS: Attachment. Completion. Perfection. Recognition. Honors. Ultimate change. Success. Triumph in undertakings. Admiration of others.
REVERSE MEANINGS: Imperfection. Failure to complete task. Lack of vision.

DEALING THE CARDS

Fortune telling using Tarot cards is a complex business. There are numerous methods of laying out the cards, and the meaning of each card differs according to its relationship with the others. Here is one simple method cartomancers use to test their skill and intuition.

To READ A FORTUNE in the Tarot, the complete 78-card pack can be used, but the process is generally easier and quicker if you employ just the 22 Major Arcana. In the examples that follow, we have presented just one of the many possible methods, called the Ten-Card Spread, using the traditional Marseilles Tarot deck.

First, the questioner and the diviner, or Tarot reader, sit facing each other across a table. The diviner then arranges the cards, all the same way up, in numerical sequence, beginning with The Fool and ending with XXI The World. Clearing his or her mind of all other thoughts, the questioner concentrates on a specific problem and states it aloud to the diviner. At the same time the questioner shuffles the deck face down. The method of shuffling is unimportant, but it must be done by the questioner.

Positive and negative
When this has been done, the questioner places the deck face down in front of the diviner. The diviner then turns over the first six cards and places them face up on the table in the sequence shown in the diagram opposite, turning them over sideways rather than lengthwise so that each one is the same way up as it was placed by the questioner. This is very important, since those cards that the diviner views right way up represent a strong, positive reading, and those that are upside down are said to be inverted, and therefore have a weak, delayed, or even opposite meaning. If, however, the first card or more than half the cards are inverted, the diviner may feel that reversing all of them (so that inverted cards face the right way up and *vice versa*) results in a more accurate reading.

The next step is to explore the individual meaning of the six exposed cards:

Card 1: Present position
This card refers to the general atmosphere in which the questioner is presently living and working. It also represents the questioner.

Card 2: Immediate influence
This card is said to cross the questioner (that is, it is placed across the previous card) and deals with influences that lie just ahead in time.

Card 3: Goal or destiny
This card crowns the questioner (it lies above Card 1) and symbolizes his or her ultimate fate. It expresses the best that can be accomplished based on existing circumstances. It may also reflect a more immediate aim or ideal.

Card 4: Distant past foundation
This card is behind the questioner (to the right of Card 1) and shows the early events and influences on which present events are based.

Card 5: Recent past events
This card goes beneath the questioner and depicts events or spheres of influence in the recent past. It can also represent distant past influences exerting strong pressure on recent events.

Card 6: Future influence
This card lies in front of (to the left of) Card 1 and portrays influences in the near future.

> Those cards that the diviner views right way up represent a strong, positive reading, and those that are upside down have a weak, delayed, or even opposite meaning.

After these readings have been taken, the diviner turns over the next four cards from the deck, placing them one above the other in a vertical line to the right of the previous cards, as shown in the diagram. (The remaining 12 cards are then set aside.)

Card 7: The questioner
This card attempts to place the questioner in perspective by depicting a present position or attitude within the surrounding circumstances.

Card 8: Environmental factors
This card illustrates the questioner's position in life and effect on others, and reveals the effects of his or her relationships.

Card 9: Inner emotions
This card portrays the secret hopes, desires, fears, and anxieties of the questioner, and points to the feelings he or she will have in the future. It may also symbolize ulterior motives.

Card 10: Final results
This card depicts the results of all the influences revealed in the other cards, provided the important events and forces remain the same.

Relationships between the cards
After reading the individual cards, the diviner should go back and interpret them as they relate to each other. Card 9, for example, frequently offers an insight into the questioner's underlying fears and anxieties, which may help to explain the significance of the other cards. The relationship between the cards might indicate a trend or pattern, reveal a changing life plan, or indicate the appropriate direction in which the questioner should be heading.

The future in ten cards

Most packs of Tarot cards include printed definitions of the meaning of each card in both its upright and reversed position. It is quite a straightforward task to use this information to interpret how the cards lie in the Ten-Card Spread.

Goal or destiny

3

Final results

10

LE BATELEUR
THE MAGICIAN

Inner emotions

9

LA LUNE
THE MOON

Future influence

6

L'AMOUREUX
THE LOVER

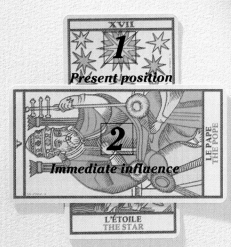

Present position

1

Immediate influence

2

L'ÉTOILE
THE STAR

LE PAPE
THE POPE

Distant past foundation

4

L'EMPEREUR
THE EMPEROR

Environmental factors

8

LA ROUE DE FORTUNE
THE WHEEL OF FORTUNE

Recent past events

5

LE CHARIOT
THE CHARIOT

The questioner

7

LE MONDE
THE WORLD

SAMPLE READINGS

The sample readings given here should give you some idea how the interpretation of the cards can be influenced by the nature of the question and questioner, and the position of the cards in the spread.

3

1

2

6

10

9

8

4

7

5

Card 2: Immediate influence
This card, VIII Justice, confirms that the questioner's present concern is with her relationship with the older man.

Card 3: Goal or destiny
XVIIII The Sun here clearly indicates the young woman's need and desire for companionship and marriage.

Cards 4 and 5: Distant past foundation and Recent past events
XVIII The Moon and VIIII The Hermit in these positions reveal the deception in the woman's previous marriage and her caution about any future marriage plans.

Card 6: Future influence
The Fool here confirms that the questioner sometimes displays poor judgment and a lack of discipline. She is young, adventurous, and lacks restraint.

Reading No. 1
The questioner is a young woman who is recently divorced and has custody of her two-year-old daughter. The questioner currently dates an older man who has asked her to marry him. She feels that she married foolishly the first time. She asks if the outlook is more favorable for marriage the second time around.

Card 1: Present position
The card here, XIIII Temperance, confirms the questioner's concern about making any new changes in her life. She must be more cautious before making any future rash decisions.

Card 7: The questioner
XII The Hanged Man in this position reveals the current period of suspension and transition in the questioner's life.

Card 8: Environmental factors
X The Wheel of Fortune here confirms the existence of the new relationship and the possibility of eventual remarriage — for good or bad.

Card 9: Inner emotions
When laid down this card appears upside down, thereby giving it a reverse meaning. V The Pope in this position suggests that the woman is vulnerable, and tends to repeat mistakes.

Card 10: Final results
XV The Devil in this position clearly indicates that marriage with the new acquaintance would prove disastrous for the questioner. She would find herself unhappy and in a subservient situation without love or understanding.

Card 3: Goal or destiny
This card appears upside down, giving it a reverse meaning. XV The Devil in this position confirms that the questioner is going to be relieved of work pressures.

Card 4: Distant past foundation
IIII The Emperor reveals the existence of a strong paternal influence in past years that has been a guiding light, but has prompted defiance.

Card 5: Recent past events
VII The Chariot indicates that sometimes the questioner makes snap judgments that can cause some problems within the family or at work.

Card 6: Future influence
VI The Lover in this position shows that the questioner and his wife will enjoy companionship in retirement.

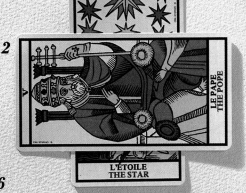

3

1

2

4

10

9

8

7

Reading No. 2
A middle-aged man seeks advice on several pressing questions, including the status of a 15-year-old third marriage, plans for retirement, and the outlook for relationships with relatives and in-laws.

Card 1: Present position
XVII The Star indicates the questioner believes the current atmosphere is favorable for close companionship in retirement.

Card 2: Immediate influence
V The Pope here suggests domination by obligations and rituals, especially in-laws and other relatives, which has caused some friction within the family.

5

Card 7: The questioner
XXI The World here suggests that the questioner is in a favorable position in his present job.

Card 8: Environmental factors
X The Wheel of Fortune indicates the strong influence the questioner exerts on other people through his success and good fortune.

Card 9: Inner emotions
XVIII The Moon falling in this place reveals for the first time the fears and anxieties of the questioner, and indicates that he has a tendency to manipulate other people.

Card 10: Final results
I The Magician here confirms that the questioner is a person of resourcefulness and creativity. He is capable of achieving a rewarding marriage and a happy retirement, plus good relationships with relatives and in-laws.

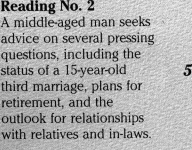

CHAPTER SIX

BODY OF BELIEF

Physiognomists and palmists would have us believe that we each carry on our bodies the telltale signs of our character, temperament, and even of our ultimate destinies.

In Shakespeare's play *Macbeth*, Duncan, king of Scotland, announces: "There's no art to find the mind's construction in the face." But in Shakespeare's day there was indeed such an art. The belief that the appearance of the face and the shape of every part of the body — including even the moles on it — revealed the soul, character, and "mind's construction" was popular from the Middle Ages onward. These traditions, originating in ancient Greek and Roman literature, went by the general name of physiognomy.

This art, which sought the inner meaning of things from outer appearances, was

HEARTS AND EARS

If you have a deep diagonal crease in one or both earlobes you may be vulnerable to heart disease. That was the finding of a research team headed by Edgar Lichstein at the Mount Sinai School of Medicine in New York in 1974. Among 531 heart attack patients admitted to the hospital with acute heart attack, almost half had such an earlobe crease, compared with only 30 percent in a disease-free group.

Two years later the same team performed another study, this time on over 100 post-mortem cases. The corpses with earlobe creases showed significantly worse hardening of the coronary arteries than those without.

Genetic factors

Opinions vary as to why these creases occur. One theory is that they result from degeneration of the elastic substances around the tiny arteries of the earlobe. Dr. Roger Williams, of the University of Utah, suspected that they were due to genetic factors but has failed to establish this in his research. Dr. Williams suggests that the creases may be caused by people sleeping on their sides. This habit can hamper breathing and might trigger a heart attack.

A typical tippler
This man's coarse features and red cheeks spoke volumes to the physiognomist. According to a book by the 17th-century physiognomist Johann Lavater, this is the face of a drunkard.

especially popular in the late Middle Ages because, unlike astrology or necromancy, it was not involved at first with the prediction of future events, which was frowned on by the church. Nor was physiognomy based on occult theories concerning spiritual beings, the music of the spheres, the stars, or planetary movements; rather it was knowledge derived from direct observation. It was therefore classified as natural magic, rather than the complex celestial or diabolical magic of which the church disapproved.

However, the church's censure did not stop physiognomists from beginning to treat their art as an occult science and using it as a basis for divination of

---

A man who was judged to look like a bull was believed to be stubborn, earthy, and even violent.

---

future events. They made prophecies based upon the appearance of the face, the nature and number of crease lines on the forehead, the size and color of the nails on the hands and feet, and the positions of moles on the body. By the 16th century, even handwriting, elementary kinds of body language, and different types of laughter (in the occult science known as gelotoscopia) were being used as the basis for divination.

Astrological links

Among the large number of medieval occult sciences of this kind, the most popular were undoubtedly the sister arts of physiognomy and palmistry. They both had their roots in the classical world of Greece and Rome. By the 16th century, however, physiognomy was widely spread throughout Europe and had become closely linked with the most intellectual of all Western occult sciences: astrology.

One of the leading physiog-nomists in the 15th century was the Italian Bartholomaeus Cocles, who was also a prominent palmist. The illustrations to

A bullish face
This 19th-century print is based on Johann Lavater's sketches of a bovine personality two centuries earlier.

Cocles's extensive texts on physiognomy are quaint by modern standards, and make rather obvious points. The art of physiognomy is essentially based on a codification of what any sensible person might well take for granted — that the outer appearance of a person is to some degree an indicator of his or her inner disposition. What distinguishes physiognomy from mere common sense, however, is its link to astrology, and to the zodiacal, or planetary, traditions.

Animal characteristics

Another line of thought that enriched the science of physiognomy was the notion that certain human faces resembled animal forms. A person's appearance was taken at face value, so a man who was judged to look like a bull was believed to be stubborn, earthy, and violent, and a man with a face like a monkey was thought to be a chatterbox and a thief.

The art of metoposcopy, the study of forehead lines, was more complicated. Although known in the medieval world, this art did not really become popular until the 17th century, with the publication of Jerome Cardan's exhaustive *Metoposcopia*. This laid down the fanciful notion that the seven main frontal lines were linked with the seven known planets of our solar system. Minute deviations and cross-lines on the main frontal lines led to dramatic interpretations. For example, Cardan claimed that a single cross on the line associated with Mars denoted a person of wanton morals who might meet a violent death through one of the Martian instruments — iron, steel, or fire.

The meaning of moles

Facial spots and moles found on the body were also subject to somewhat complex interpretations according to astrological principles, although the emphasis was on zodiacal, rather than planetary, influences. *Physiognomie, and Chiromancie, Metoposcopie*, written by the English palmist and astrologer Richard Saunders in 1653, gives over 80 positions for moles and explains how to interpret their position in each case.

READING A FACE

Popular literature of the 15th and 16th centuries demonstrates a simple approach to physiognomy. Seven distinct facial types were associated with the natures of the seven planets known at that time. The angular, intense face of the soldier was linked with the forthright, martial quality of Mars. The well-proportioned, dignified, and beautiful face was seen as an expression of the creative and benign warmth of the sun. The alert, sometimes shifty face of the beggar, and the sensitive, refined face of the artist, were both associated with the planet Mercury. The round, white, bloated face, with large eyes, deeply lidded, was linked with the moon. The sallow, gaunt, ugly face, with prominent bones and stringy neck, was seen as the expression of dark Saturn. The plump face of the stereotypical well-fed priest was linked with the benevolence and cultural sophistication of Jupiter. The sensuous face of an attractive woman was a sign of the lascivious and earthy side of Venus. Such planetary stereotypes are to be found everywhere in the literature and art of the late medieval period.

Planetary influence

This illustration is based on a print from Jean Belot's Oeuvres *(1649), showing the areas of planetary influence on the face. It differs from early tradition in assigning the left eye to Venus and the nose to the Moon.*

Planets on the face

Each planetary influence could be traced on the face, although there were a number of systems, and they tended to differ from one physiognomist to another. An early tradition linked the right eye with the Sun, the left eye with the Moon, the forehead with Mars, the right ear with Jupiter, the left ear with Saturn, the mouth with Mercury, and Venus with the skin.

Lines on the forehead

The rules followed by experts such as the 17th-century Italian physiognomist Filippo Finella are more complex. For example, in the study of frontal lines (metoposcopy), the line of Mars that stretches across the forehead in a continuous line denotes both courage and a warlike disposition. But if that line is broken, then the person is revealed as a quarrelsome brawler, who will be unfortunate in warfare. Similarly, if the line of the moon is clear and long in its course above the eyebrow, then this indicates that the subject has an over-active imagination and a tendency to travel to exotic places. Should there be a break in this line, however, it indicates a somewhat capricious and untruthful nature. Besides writing on physiognomy and chiro-mancy, Finella published three books in 1633, known collectively as *Libri Tres Naevorum* (*Three Books of Moles*), each dealing with 100 cases of moles on the face, neck, and head, in terms of location, color, and relationships to other moles.

The lore of moles, as set out by Finella, is both complex and precise. A mole on the left forehead, below the moon line is, for example, a sign of petulance and lust.

A similar mole at the end of the moon line indicates that the person will be prosecuted because of murder or homicide. Should that mole be red, then the owner is advised to be wary of his or her own kin; and if it is black, then this is supposedly a sign that he or she will be tortured.

Frontal lines

This woodcut from Cardan's Metoposcopia *(1658) illustrates the rulerships of the seven planets over the seven main forehead lines. The planets are, from the top: Saturn, Jupiter, Mars, the Sun, Venus, Mercury, and the Moon.*

Saturne.

Jupiter

mars

Le soleil

uenus

mercure

La lune

PALMISTRY

Fortune telling from an examination of the hands was originally regarded as a respectable science. Yet in recent centuries it has been dismissed by most authorities as superstitious mumbo-jumbo. Now the scientific establishment is beginning to consider that palmistry may actually have a rational basis.

Chiromantic woodcut
The unbroken line of Saturn that runs down the center of this palm indicates prosperity in its owner.

*P*ALMISTRY HAS BEEN DIVIDED by its practitioners over the centuries into two different forms, which, while being closely related, are very different in both tradition and application. One division is called chirognomy, and is based on the study of the form of the hand — its shape and length, its elasticity, the quality of the fingers, the shape of the palm, and so on. The other division is called chiromancy, and concerns itself with the study of the lines and papillary ridges on the palm and fingers.

Chiromancy

The word *chiromancy* is derived from two Greek words, which mean "telling the future from the hand." The majority of palmists who are interested in predicting events from the hand rely upon this aspect of palmistry, devoted exclusively to the study of lines. Almost all

---

Modern palm readers study the hand as a guide to temperament, psychological patterns, and mental states.

---

forms of early palmistry were concerned mainly with chiromancy, and most of the important books on palmistry provided configurations of palm lines set in drawings of hands that were identical in shape, showing how little interest early palmists paid to the actual form of the hand.

Chirognomy

Modern palmistry has almost completely reversed the ancient tradition, and nowadays palmists place great emphasis on the form of the hand, on what is called chirognomy. Modern palm readers are interested in studying the hand as a guide to temperament, psychological patterns, and mental states.

The 15th-century Italian palmist and physiognomist Bartholomaeus Cocles belonged to the ancient chiromantic tradition, concentrating almost exclusively on the lines on the hand. By the 19th century a German doctor, Carl Gustav Carus, was using the contrasting

THE ORIGINS OF PALMISTRY

The occult literature of the past indicates that palmistry was widely practiced in many parts of the world in ancient times, but in exactly what form is not clear.

We know from Roman literature that the hand was seen as an instrument for healing. The middle finger, associated with Saturn, was called the "medical finger" because of its healing power. The Roman emperor Vespasian, who ruled A.D. 69–79, was reported to be able to heal the sick by touching them with his hand.

Learned priests

According to the ancient Greeks, chiromancy was an age-old art even in their day, for it was part of the divinatory practice of the Chaldean astrologers. Chaldea was an ancient country in southern Babylonia (what is now southern Iraq) that was finally swamped by a Persian invasion in 539 B.C. The priestly class of this state was educated in classical Babylonian literature, and renowned for its knowledge of astronomy and archeology.

The palmistry of India probably derived from these same Chaldean sources, almost 3,000 years ago. The earliest Western texts to present systematic rules by which the hand might be interpreted are medieval. The surviving manuscripts show that many of the names given to the lines of the palm reflect the ancient astrological tradition.

chirognomic approach. He attempted to relate temperament to the shape of the hand, and he showed little interest in the lines on the hand.

In his *Traité Complet de Chiromancie, Déductive et Expérimentale* (1938), the modern French palmist Georges Muchery classifies hands according to their planetary influences. There are eight types of hands, corresponding with the Sun, Mercury, Venus, Earth, the Moon, Mars, Jupiter, and Saturn. Muchery claims that the meanings associated with the lines change according to the particular form of the hand in which the lines appear.

Most palmists, however, are not concerned with establishing working systems of palmistry so much as in using what they know about the hand. Almost all modern palmistry is practiced in the same vein as in the past — mainly as an exercise in intuition. Some modern palmists have made serious attempts to resurrect the connection between astrology and palmistry, on the basis that they both represent personality and destiny. They have linked

Madame Nordica
The illustrious prima donna, whose gift of a silver cigarette case saved Cheiro's life.

Louis Hamon — "Cheiro"

CHEIRO
One of the most famous palmists was Louis Hamon, who called himself Cheiro. He was born in Wicklow, Ireland, in 1866 and died in 1936 in Hollywood, California, where he was working as a scriptwriter and as an author specializing in numerology, palmistry, and prediction.

The fate of royalty
One of Cheiro's books, *World Prediction* (1928), was a bestseller. It is, however, remarkable for its lack of accurate predictions of future world events. Yet Cheiro seems to have had the knack of foretelling personal fates. For example, he predicted the date of the death of Queen Victoria, the exact month of the death of Edward VII, and the execution of the czar of Russia.

Cheiro claimed to have studied palmistry in India for four years, consulting a palmistic treatise written in a mysterious red ink on human skin. But there is no trace of this arcane Indian lore in his own writings: nothing in his books suggests that he had anything but a passing familiarity with the European tradition.

Clairvoyant vision
Many of Cheiro's adages about the meanings of the lines are derived from medieval writers. He based his classification of hand types on the work of the 19th-century French palmist Count Casimir D'Arpentigny, whose research he adopted without acknowledgment. Cheiro did not appear to have any real understanding of his chosen method of clairvoyance but he was gifted with more than his fair share of Irish blarney.

He also had a feel for publicity. In his extensive world travels, he usually managed to get the press on his side. In 1894, for example, the *Boston Budget* claimed: "Cheiro, the Palmist, is one of the most remarkable scientists that the world has ever known." In a long article in the *New York World*, in November 1893, a journalist recorded how he tested Cheiro's abilities. He reported that, in one session at which he was present, the palmist described the life and characteristics of each person there with the most wonderful accuracy, "without knowing either the names or the positions in life of any of the people, and without asking a question or any beating about the bush."

Cheiro made his interpretations from the impressions made by hands on smoked paper. Many of the more important hands from his collections were preserved for posterity in his books.

A dangerous game
The handprint he preserved of Madame Nordica, who was in her day a famous prima donna, had special significance for Cheiro. His gift, besides bringing him both fame and notoriety, also made him enemies, and several attempts were made on his life. During one of his many visits to New York, where he mingled with the cream of society, predicting their rise and fall with apparent ease, he advised a young lady to break with her lover, on the grounds that the liaison boded ill. When the young man heard of this, he called upon Cheiro, pretending that he was seeking a consultation, and tried to stab him in the heart.

Fortunately, the blow was deflected by a silver cigarette case given to Cheiro by Madame Nordica, and he escaped serious injury. Cheiro did not indicate whether or not he had foreseen the attack!

A helping hand
Cheiro took impressions of his clients' hands on smoked paper. This is the hand of Madame Nordica.

personal horoscope figures with handprints, echoing an attempt first made by the German palmist Johann Rothmann in a seminal work of the late 16th century.

In modern times medical researchers have been attempting to put the art of hand-interpretation on a scientific footing. Most work has been done on dermatoglyphics, the scientific term for the study of fingerprints, or, more broadly, the ridged patterns on the skin of the hands and feet. Over 40 disorders, ranging from Down's syndrome to prenatal German measles, have been linked with abnormal palm prints.

> ## Over 40 disorders, ranging from Down's syndrome to prenatal German measles, have been linked with abnormal palm prints.

There have been a number of interesting exploratory projects in this field. Dr. Charlotte Wolff's book *The Hand in Psychological Diagnosis* (1951) documents her extensive work on the relationship between mental diseases and hand forms. In *The Hand of Man* (1933) one of the pioneers in this field, the English medical researcher Dr. Noel Jaquin, publicized his findings on the correlation between certain diseases and specific patterns of lines on the palms. Jaquin produced micro-photographs of

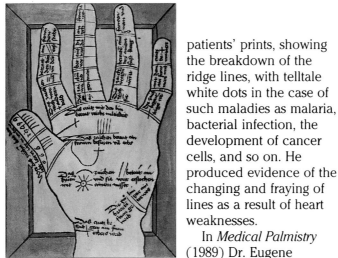

The Art of Chiromancy
This plate is from the earliest printed work on palmistry, produced by Johann Hartlieb in around 1475.

patients' prints, showing the breakdown of the ridge lines, with telltale white dots in the case of such maladies as malaria, bacterial infection, the development of cancer cells, and so on. He produced evidence of the changing and fraying of lines as a result of heart weaknesses.

In *Medical Palmistry* (1989) Dr. Eugene Scheimann, a physician from Chicago, describes how he has used palm examination in medical diagnosis for over 50 years. He believes that it is a reliable aid to determining genetic make-up and susceptibility to hormonal imbalances.

The fringes of medicine
Walter Sorell, in his book, *The Study of the Human Hand* (1967), supported the connection between the appearance of the hand and the subject's state of health. Sorell pointed out that an egg-shaped island on the Life line was sometimes a sign of the onset of cancer.

Modern research continues to pursue the study of the hand on a scientific basis. Perhaps the ancient arts of chirognomy and chiromancy will resume their former position on the fringes of mainstream medicine?

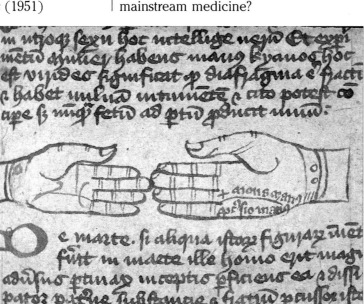

Healing hands
Medieval doctors knew that a patient's hands often held diagnostic clues. This illustration is from an English medical treatise of the 15th century.

LIFE LINES
Research on embryos has shown that the first line to develop on the hand is the Life line. Palmists have noted that, along with the other lines on the hand, it continues to develop during the subject's life. In his book, *The Study of the Human Hand*, Walter Sorell produced prints of the same person at the age of 9 and 29; they clearly show developments in both the Head and Life lines. The degree of change is said to indicate alterations in the psyche and destiny of the subject.

What are the implications of this for palmistry? Such changes support the views of many modern palmists and astrologers, that fate, as revealed in the hand or the horoscope, can be altered by exercising the will. This is an ancient concept, reflected in, for example, the *I Ching*.

Herald of doom
It is a palmistic tradition that the length of the Life line may be taken as an indicator of the length of life. In *The Science of the Hand* (1886), the palmist Edward Heron-Allen wrote: "The line ceasing abruptly with a few little parallel lines...is an indication of sudden death. If the line is continually crossed by little cutting bars, it is an indication of continual, but not severe, illnesses. If the line is broken inside a square...it indicates recovery from a serious illness; a square always denotes protection from some danger."

Modern medical research conducted at the Bristol Royal Infirmary in England in 1990 reportedly confirms this principle. Dr. Paul Newrick measured the Life lines on both hands of 100 corpses. The length of the Life lines on the right hands, Newrick found, bore a statistical correlation to the actual length of the subjects' lives.

HAND OF FORTUNE

The hand has long been regarded as an indicator of an individual's personality and temperament. The image of the hand has also been used as a sacred symbol by diverse cultures throughout the world. It may be that these civilizations discovered, by observation over the centuries, the fundamental truth behind the maxim: "The future lies in the palm of your hand."

Arab amulets

L'ART DE LIRE DANS LES LIGNES DE LA MAIN 5 fr

RASCETTES

DIY hand-reading

The Hand of Fatima

The hand's importance as a magical symbol in Arabic culture is clear from the popularity of an amulet called the Hand of Fatima, which is still worn in modern times. Traditionally, the symbolism of this hand is linked with Islam. The thumb represents the Prophet Mohammed, the index finger his daughter Fatima, the middle finger her husband Ali, and so on. However, the existence of such hand amulets predates Islam.

Popular palmistry

Palmistry enjoyed a resurgence of popularity in the Western world in the early 20th century. This book cover is from a French guide to the subject, published about 1920.

Roman bronze

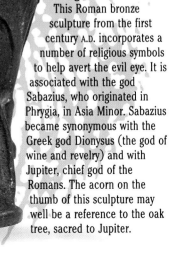

"Fortune hunting"

A skeptical sketch

This is an early 19th-century satirical view of palmistry entitled "Fortune hunting" by the English cartoonist James Gillray. It is the gypsy palmists rather than their huntsmen clients who are more likely to find their fortunes — by picking the pockets of their customers.

Magic hand

This Roman bronze sculpture from the first century A.D. incorporates a number of religious symbols to help avert the evil eye. It is associated with the god Sabazius, who originated in Phrygia, in Asia Minor. Sabazius became synonymous with the Greek god Dionysus (the god of wine and revelry) and with Jupiter, chief god of the Romans. The acorn on the thumb of this sculpture may well be a reference to the oak tree, sacred to Jupiter.

Hopewell Indian ornament

A grave hand
This larger-than-lifesize hand was found in the grave of an American Indian of the Hopewell Culture in Ohio. It is over 1,500 years old and is made of mica. This artifact was possibly of some spiritual or material value, since it was discovered over 400 miles from the nearest source of mica.

Memorial plaques

Hands of the faithful
These representations of palm prints can be found at the city palace at Bikaner, Rajasthan, in northwest India. They are memorials to faithful Hindu wives who were sacrificed on their husband's funeral pyre. This practice, known as suttee, has now been outlawed in India.

Indian symbols
The hand was a powerful shamanistic symbol in some American Indian cults. Hand impressions have been found among the petroglyphs in the sacred sites of Indians in Arizona and Utah. Many of these are linked with animal pictures dealing with hunting, and it has been suggested that the hand paintings have a magical significance. Research has indicated that the Navajo and Hopi Indians created such pictures as salutations to the Great Spirit.

Hopewell Indian pot

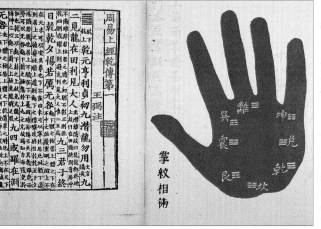

Diagram from the I Ching

Chinese palmistry
The basic diagram of the palm used in Chinese occult science is said to be at least 2,000 years old. In this system the palm is divided into eight areas, or "palaces," each associated directly with one of the eight trigrams that form the backbone of the predictive system of the *I Ching*. The Chinese system of "palaces" corresponds quite closely to the European system.

READING YOUR HAND

Modern palmists use a number of different systems to tell fortunes and predict the future from the study of the hand.

DIGIT DETAILS
Palmists glean basic information about a person from a close examination of the fingers.

Revealing fingers
The thumb (the finger of willpower) indicates an individual's feelings of self-worth, palmists suggest. People with large thumbs as well as those with small thumbs may have difficulties with personal relationships; they are either dominating or dominated. A medium-sized thumb makes for a well-balanced personality.

The Jupiter, or index, finger represents an individual's view of his or her standing in the world. A short index finger may indicate low self-esteem, whereas an extra-long index finger may be a sign of a superiority complex.

The Saturn, or middle, finger is interpreted as being the balancing mechanism between the opposite sides of the hand that reveal the conscious and the intuitive parts of its owner's psyche. If the finger is very long, it can indicate a depressive personality, whereas a short middle finger can suggest an irresponsible person.

Signs of happiness
The Apollo, or ring, finger reveals an individual's inner happiness and fulfillment. A straight and well-developed finger indicates an outgoing person. If the finger is very long, it indicates emotions that lie too close to the surface.

The Mercury, or little, finger is associated with all modes of communication. If this finger is straight and reaches to the first knuckle of the Apollo finger, then this person has a good intuition about developing relationships with others.

*R*EADING THE LINES ON PALMS has been a method of character analysis since ancient times. Modern palmists, however, claim that they can construct a more accurate picture of an individual's life by examining the whole hand, and taking note of details such as the size, shape, and color. They argue that reading hands is a more revealing method of divination than drawing up a person's horoscope.

Palmists say it is essential to examine both hands to obtain the fullest reading. The consensus among modern palmists is that an individual's dominant hand reveals the conscious and objective self, and the non-dominant hand reveals the subconscious and subjective self. Palmists also claim that analyzing both hands reveals the potential every individual has to influence certain areas in his or her life.

Hand shapes
Many palmists categorize hands using a system developed by the 19th-century French chiromancer Count Casimir D'Arpentigny, who classified the hand into seven basic shapes. He also set out the characteristics that have become associated with such hands.

The elementary hand is short-fingered and large-palmed and may indicate a person who is a slow thinker, according to D'Arpentigny. The square hand is as broad as it is long; it reveals someone who is practical and logical thinking. The spatulate hand is spade-shaped and straight-edged; it indicates an enthusiastic personality.

The philosophical hand has knotty and heavy-jointed fingers that indicate an intellectual cast of mind. The conic hand has long, tapering fingers and indicates a sensitive and creative personality. The psychic hand is usually long and slim and often has a slightly crooked little finger; this hand indicates someone with psychic abilities. The mixed hand combines one or two elements of the other types; the owner of this hand will display a mixture of tendencies.

The Life line
Many palmists believe the Life line does not necessarily show an individual's allotted span of life but indicates a person's level of vitality. The line usually runs from midway between the Jupiter finger and the thumb down and around the mount of Venus. A long and clear line indicates a strong constitution. A Life line broken in places can be a warning of health problems.

Although the Life line may not actually indicate when a person will die, it does reveal how long the

> The consensus among modern palmists is that an individual's dominant hand reveals the conscious and objective self, and the nondominant hand reveals the subconscious and subjective self.

The map of life
Palmists believe that the lines on the hand provide a guide to every individual's personal destiny.

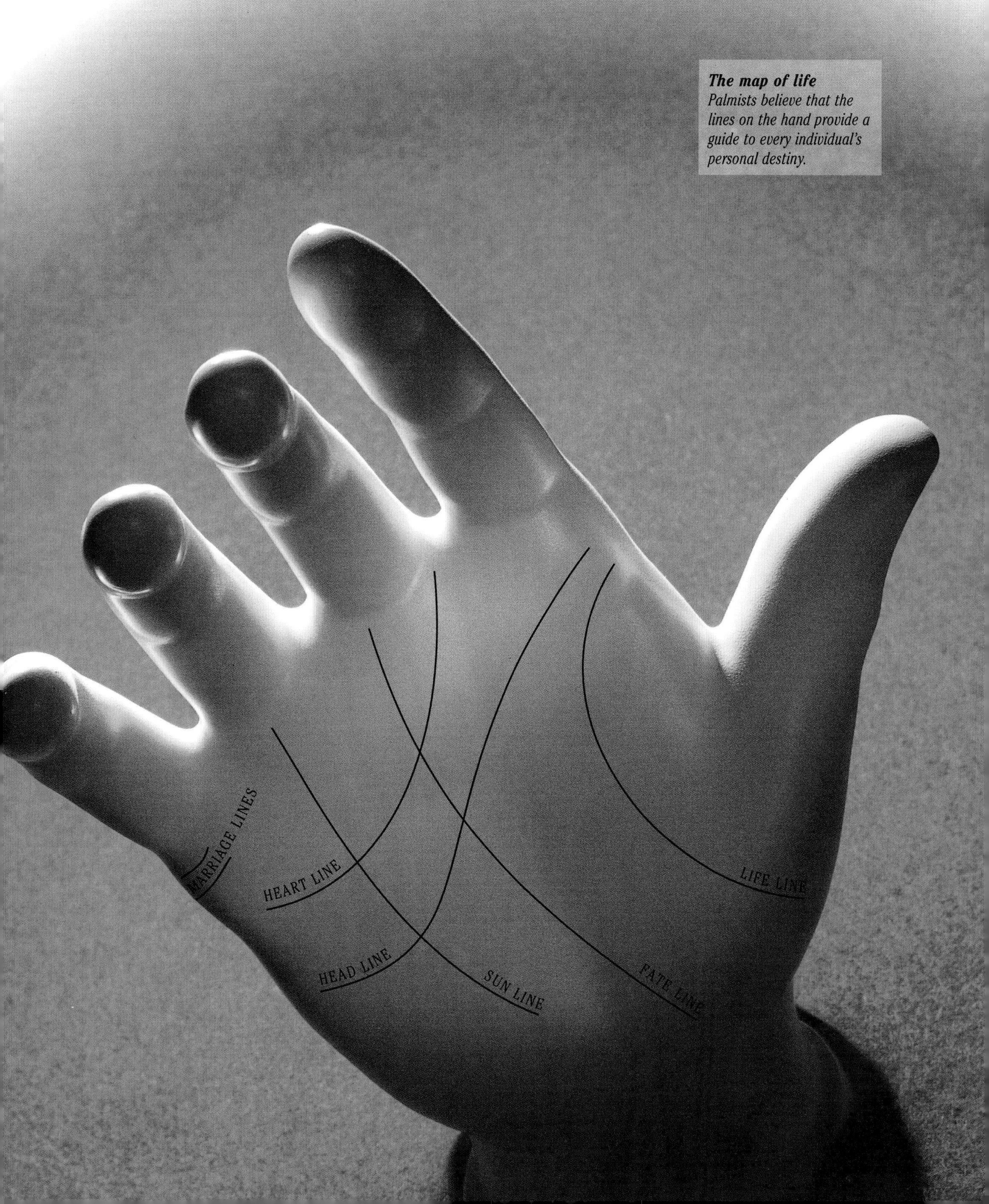

MARRIAGE LINES

HEART LINE

HEAD LINE

SUN LINE

FATE LINE

LIFE LINE

Benito Mussolini

MAN OF IRON

Palmists are understandably reluctant to predict a client's early death. However, in 1935, the palmist Josef Ranald told the Italian dictator Benito Mussolini that he had only two years to live.

Ranald wrote: "His line of heart, running up to the base of the second finger, revealed to me an almost morbid disposition and great egocentricity; while a branch curved out of this line to join it to the head line in definite indication of temper and ruthlessness. Closer examination showed the lines of life and head to be broken in many places. But, strangely enough, every break but one seemed mended by a square."

Misleading lines

The handprint showed the breaks in the lines supported by tiny squares. These are protective signs, indicating that an individual will overcome difficulties. But the Life line of the dictator's hand was distinctly shorter than one would expect in such a powerful personality. Ranald concluded that Mussolini would die in 1937, at the age of 54, and informed the dictator of what he saw. In fact, Mussolini was executed by Italian partisans in 1945.

Other palmists, no doubt with the benefit of hindsight, have attempted to explain Ranald's mistake. It appears, they say, that he read the single break in the Life line not accompanied by a square — rather than the end of the Life line itself — as indicating Mussolini's death.

individual should be able to sustain life. It is sensible to compare the Life line in both hands. The dominant hand will show the influences that have a bearing on an individual's life and the other hand will reveal the genetic inheritance.

The Head line

The Head line, palmists say, is the main indicator of intelligence. It begins at the side of the hand below the index finger and extends across the plain of Mars. The length and the slant of the line can vary enormously from hand to hand. If the line is clearly marked and deeply etched, it indicates a powerful and vigorous intelligence.

The length of the Head line indicates mental capacity. A short Head line can indicate limited intelligence. If the Head line is long and reaches across the palm, it indicates intellectual and imaginative potential. Albert Einstein, for example, had a Head line that extended almost all the way across his palm, demonstrating great intelligence.

The Heart line

The Heart line, today's experts say, indicates the emotional life of an individual. This line runs above the Head line, starting near or under the Jupiter finger. The Heart line should be clearly marked without being too thin or broad. A pink line indicates a strong cardiovascular system. A thin Heart line may indicate emotional coldness. If the line is blurred, this can indicate emotional difficulties. If the Heart line is crossed with branches, it shows a vivid and lively personality with many romantic encounters and attachments. Branches breaking upward are usually interpreted as signifying successful attachments. Branches breaking downward signify unsatisfactory liaisons that do not last.

D'Arpentigny's hand system
The seven types of handshape are, clockwise from the top: conic, mixed, philosophic, spatulate, square, psychic, and elementary.

The Fate line

The Fate line, or the line of Saturn, runs up the center of the palm toward the mount of Saturn. This line varies enormously from person to person, and it is sometimes entirely absent from an individual's hand.

The Fate line can indicate what control an individual has taken of his or her life. It also shows the path a person's career takes. If the line is clear and unbroken, and travels from the wrist right up to the mount of Saturn, this indicates a brilliant and successful career. A break on the Fate line shows a sudden disruption in a career that will last as long as the break continues. Short bars across the Fate line represent obstacles to be overcome.

The Sun line

The Sun line, or the line of Apollo, is a vertical line that runs up the palm toward the mount of Apollo. A clearly marked straight and unbroken Sun line indicates good fortune, fame, and happiness. Sometimes the Sun line is short in length and starts at the Heart line. This can indicate good fortune that begins with the right personal relationship. The Sun line is a very protective sign. If it is absent, however lucky the other lines, the subject will meet with setbacks.

Marriage lines

Small transverse lines that lie on the side of the hand between the base of the little finger and the Heart line and run into the mount of Mercury are called the marriage, or relationship, lines. Such lines are luckiest if they are pink and unbroken. Their lengths are related to the length of each relationship. Short vertical lines rising from the relationship lines indicate children: faint lines for girls, and deep, clear lines for boys.

MOUNTS AND MARKINGS

The system of ascribing planetary names to certain areas of the palm has not changed for thousands of years.

THE PALM IS DIVIDED into seven different areas, or mounts, each of which is named after one of the seven planets used in astrology. Palmists interpret the shape, size, color, feel, and texture of these mounts as revealing much about an individual's strengths and weaknesses.

Venus

A well-rounded, firm, and healthy pink mount of Venus indicates physical vitality and a healthy sex drive. An overdeveloped Venus mount can indicate a tendency to excess.

Moon

The mount of the Moon represents a person's mental alertness and creative powers. If overdeveloped, it indicates someone who is prone to anxiety and has an overactive imagination. If the mount is underdeveloped, it indicates someone who is a conformist.

Mars

The middle part of the palm is ruled by the planet Mars and is further divided into lower and upper mounts. The mount of Mars is associated with how capable an individual is at overcoming life's adversities. A red and round lower mount indicates a person with a great will to succeed. A prominently developed upper mount can indicate a very stubborn nature.

Jupiter

A mount of Jupiter that is a low, rounded protrusion, firm to the touch and pale in color, indicates a warm, sociable, and good-natured personality. If it is underdeveloped, it indicates a person who is selfish, lazy, and inconsiderate. An overdeveloped mount of Jupiter can indicate someone who is arrogant and overambitious.

Saturn

The mount of Saturn indicates a person who is cautious and serious-minded. If the mount is overdeveloped, it is an indication of inner turmoil. If it is underdeveloped, it indicates an unremarkable person. An overdeveloped mount of Saturn can also be the sign of a depressive personality.

Apollo

A mount of Apollo (also known as the Sun mount) that is rounded, firm, and pink in color indicates a friendly, outgoing personality. A prominent mount indicates an individual who may be egotistical and vain. A flat Apollo mount indicates a dull and somewhat introspective personality.

Mercury

A low, gently rounded Mercury mount indicates that an individual has a quick wit and can be persuasive. If over-developed, it indicates selfishness. If underdeveloped the subject may be dull and uncommunicative.

SIGNS ON THE LINES

Certain markings that are sometimes found on the mounts of the hand are signs of exceptional good fortune.

The star

A star on the mount of Jupiter indicates great honors; on Saturn it can indicate great wisdom; on Apollo it signifies wealth and fame; a star on Mercury shows great success in business.

The trident

If the Heart line ends in a trident, this indicates good fortune. If the Head line ends with a trident, this is a sign of exceptional mental powers. On the Life line, a trident indicates a long and happy life.

The square

This marking is very protective if it surrounds a negative marking such as a break on a palm line. The square neutralizes any negative effect.

The triangle

This is always a lucky sign, symbolizing good fortune, peace, and harmony. On the mount of Saturn a triangle signifies an innate interest in mystical matters. On the mount of Apollo it shows artistic success. On the mount of Mercury it indicates achievements in the political arena.

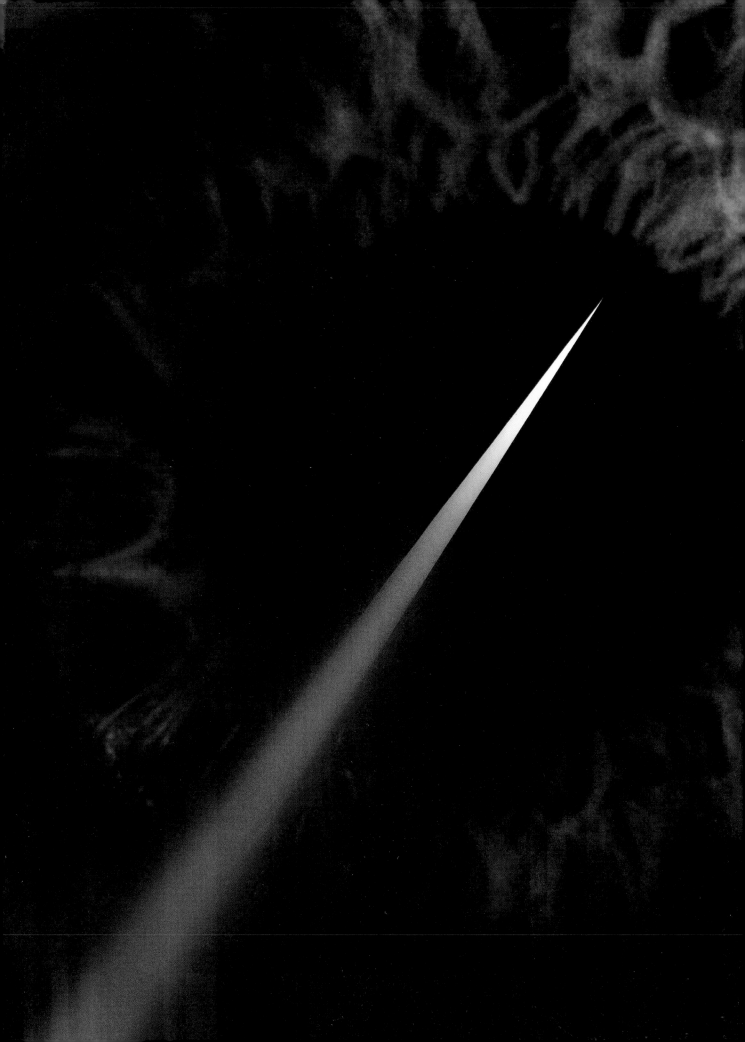

CHAPTER SEVEN

TRAVELING IN TIME

To be sure of discovering the future you would need to travel there and see it for yourself. Time travel has always been a favorite theme of science fiction but is still far from becoming a scientific fact.

Many of us at one time or another have probably indulged in a fantasy of traveling backward or forward through time — and what an array of destinations! For no vacation trip on the present-day earth, however exotic, could possibly match the excitement of a visit to ancient Rome in the days of the Emperor Augustus or to the Egypt of the pharaohs. Or perhaps would-be time travelers would prefer to revisit their own childhood and meet again old friends or relatives long dead.

A voyage into the future — if such a thing were possible — would be even more astonishing and intriguing: a visit to a

Binary star system
This illustration shows a normal star and an associated black hole. A black hole is formed when a star collapses and matter is sucked in by the collapsing star's gravitational pull. The black hole is the funnel-shaped well in the grid. The immense gravitational pull of a black hole curves the fabric of spacetime, offering the possibility, in theory at least, of time travel.

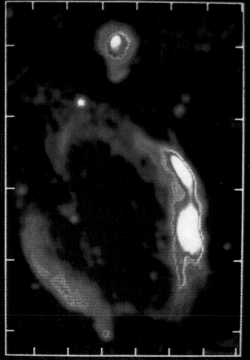

A neutron star?
The bright spot at the top of this false-color radio map is the binary star system Circinus X-1. Part of this system is so compact that it must be a neutron star or a black hole.

world of unimaginable technologies, Utopian societies, or war and catastrophe on an unprecedented scale. Science fiction has made us familiar with these possibilities, but scientists are just beginning to speculate that such fantasies might one day become reality.

Before even considering the practicalities of time travel — the prodigious challenge of constructing a real-life time machine — there are serious logical problems that have to be faced. If time travel were possible, time travelers would change the past, and also of necessity change the present from which they had come and to which they must return.

Suppose, for example, that a time traveler is transported back to the home of his maternal grandparents 60 years ago. The grandparents have just married, and his mother has not yet been born. The sudden appearance of this strangely

---

Modern physics suggests that time travel is a theoretical possibility, but only under extreme circumstances in the depths of space.

---

dressed visitor from the future in their house gives the future grandfather a terrible shock. He is an overweight 40-year-old, and the resultant heart attack kills him. The time traveler's mother will now never be born, and consequently the time traveler himself cannot exist. This must be an impossibility; yet if time travel were possible, it seems that such events might be likely to happen.

Medical breakthroughs
Travel into the future presents what is essentially the same problem, but in a slightly different form. Imagine a professor of medicine propelled 200 years into the future. He might visit a medical college and hear a lecturer explain the simple principles of the cure for all forms of cancer; a cure discovered by researchers half a century earlier and now in universal use.

Returning to the present, the professor immediately publishes this exciting information and the scourge of cancer is ended. But the cure for cancer has now been discovered 150 years earlier than in the future that the professor visited, and hundreds of thousands of individuals now live longer lives than would otherwise have been the case. This means that the whole future of the world is altered. So what has become of the future that the professor visited? Did he not visit the real future after all?

One theoretical solution to this paradox is the complex notion of "parallel universes." At its simplest, this view argues that the time traveler's intervention in the past or the future creates a whole new universe, very like the one in which the time traveler lives, but different in a few essential details. When the time traveler returns to the present, he or she goes back to a universe in which the grandfather did not die at 40. The universe in which the grandfather did die carries on in parallel, imperceptible to our senses, which are tuned in only to our own universe.

Strong gravitational pull

The discoveries of modern physics suggest that time travel is a theoretical possibility, but only under extreme circumstances in the depths of space. The most obvious candidate for an outer-space time machine is a black hole, a hypothetical star that has collapsed in upon itself — its whole immense mass squashed down to a single, small point.

It is the source of the strongest gravitational force in the universe.

Physicists have calculated that a black hole must have a bizarre effect on time because, according to Einstein's general theory of relativity, the force of gravity affects both time and space. As always with Einstein-derived theorizing about time, the effect depends totally on

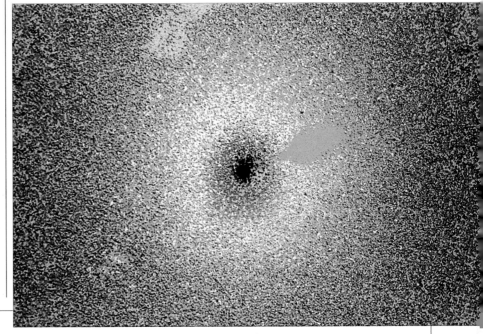

BLACK HOLES

The term *black hole* was first coined by Princeton physicist John Wheeler in 1963, but the idea is much older. The first person to anticipate the existence of a black hole in space was 18th-century French scientist Pierre-Simon Laplace. He calculated that, if a star were big enough, its gravitational field would prevent light escaping from it. Thus, he concluded: "The largest luminous bodies in the universe may be invisible."

Laplace had the general principle right, but it was not until Einstein's relativity theories that more accurate predictions could be made. In 1907 mathematician Karl Schwarzschild calculated that if a star the size of the sun collapsed to a diameter of two miles across, it would wrap time and space around it in a closed system from which nothing would ever be able to escape.

Singular stars

For many years black holes were only theoretical entities, but astronomers have now established that, as stars die, they really do collapse in on themselves under the influence of gravity. Under the right conditions,

nothing can halt this implosion until the massive star has been reduced to a point with no space and no time, known to scientists as a "singularity."

The collapsed star exerts a gravitational pull that is theoretically infinite. Not only does matter disappear down a black hole, but light is also sucked in. That is why it is called a black hole — no light escapes from it; so it is invisible.

Pierre-Simon Laplace

An unexplained explosion

Some physicists believe that there may be millions of black holes, some as small as atomic particles, others sucking in matter across thousands of light-years of space. In the constellation Cygnus, for example, a black hole is at this moment slowly eating up a giant star 20 times the size of our sun. But there has been speculation that the earth might have been struck by a mini-black hole, causing the mysterious explosion in the Tunguska region of Siberia in 1908. Most experts agree that this is unlikely. Even the impact of a miniature version would probably have swallowed up the entire earth.

Star guzzler

This is an image-processed photograph of the M87 galaxy. The black central core is made up of a cluster of stars so dense and fast-moving that experts suggest they must be in the gravitational grip of a black hole.

Parallel universes
This sci-fi magazine cover illustrates one possibility of what a time traveler might find in a parallel universe where interference with the past has changed the present — Tudor styles of dress from 16th-century England still in vogue in the 20th century. If we accept the concept of parallel universes at its most extreme, then an infinite number of universes could exist at the same time, each different in one particular aspect.

your point of view. To an observer watching from a safe distance, a spacecraft headed toward a black hole would seem to travel more and more slowly. On the brink of the black hole's "event horizon" — the edge of darkness beyond which no light can escape from the gravitational pull — the spacecraft would seem to stop altogether, hovering forever at the boundary of light.

Accelerated time
But to the crew in the spacecraft itself, the effect would be much stranger. They would experience themselves traveling very fast indeed, but events in the universe around them would be happening even faster. In theory, by the time they reached the edge of the black hole, the future of the universe to the end of time would be flashing past their eyes in a second.

After the crew was sucked into the black hole, according to some theories, an even odder experience would await them. Some physicists, such as the Australian Roy P. Kerr, believe that a spinning black hole could contain a "wormhole," leading through to another part of our own universe of spacetime, or even to a completely different universe. Emerging from the other end of the wormhole tunnel might be exactly the reverse of entering it. Whereas entering the black hole gave the crew a glimpse of the end of the universe, coming out of it

would present them with a wildly speeded-up vision of the birth of the universe. As they drew away from the hole, time effects would gradually settle down. But the crew would have moved far back in time. If the universe they emerged into was still our own, then, in this extreme example, they would gradually approach the time of their own births, which theoretically they would be able to witness from space. However, to arrive at the right time and place would

---

The spacecraft would have to be shaped somewhat like a flying saucer to resist the pressure of gravity.

---

require a feat of navigation that even a physicist might think of as being beyond the bounds of likelihood.

Black holes are, of course, extremely impractical time machines. The forces at work in their vicinity would destroy any human beings who were sucked into their gravity vortex. The atoms composing their bodies might conceivably pass through a wormhole, but only stretched out and disassembled. The experts suggest that a practical time machine in outer space would have to

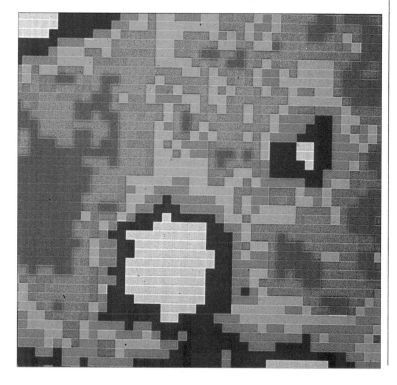

The Vela pulsar
The small white and red area on this false-color optical image is a neutron star. A spinning cylinder made up of neutron stars is a possible blueprint for a time machine in space.

exploit the distortions of time brought on by the gravity of dense bodies without forcing its time travelers actually to enter the heaviest zone.

A spinning star cylinder

Physicist Fred Alan Wolf has speculated that this might be achieved by exploiting the time zones that would exist around a spinning cylinder made up of neutron stars — stars that have collapsed in upon themselves without quite becoming black holes. A spacecraft dodging around in these time zones would theoretically be able to move through time and then emerge to make observations of the past or future.

Interestingly, Wolf believes the spacecraft would have to be shaped somewhat like a flying saucer to resist the pressure of gravity. Shifting neutron stars around to form cylinders is not a trick that is likely to be within the reach of earth technology in the near future, however, unless some more advanced travelers in time or space come to tell us how it is done.

If you do not have an intergalactic spacecraft at your disposal, practical traveling through time is an even more distant prospect. One far-fetched, but theoretically not impossible, method of time travel involves the bizarre principle of teleportation. Nonetheless, the teleportation machine appears in many science fiction stories. It supposedly works by making a top-to-toe scan of a human body, thus establishing the precise location of every molecule of which it is composed. This information is then transmitted to another place where it is used to reconstruct the body exactly as it was — with every memory and

Time warp
This diagram shows how the gravitational pull of a large planet can warp the fabric of spacetime. It is this bending of spacetime that, in theory, creates the opportunity for time travel.

psychological characteristic intact, as well as every physical feature. In effect, it would allow a person to travel almost instantaneously over huge distances, by dematerializing and rematerializing.

If communication with the future were possible — and people's experiences of premonitory dreams suggest to some enthusiasts that it is theoretically feasible — then the bodyscan information could also be transmitted forward in time. The individual could then be rematerialized not simply in another place, but also in another time. The return journey would be achieved using the same process but in reverse. The traveler would return with his or her memories — including the memories of the visit to the future — completely intact.

None of these time-travel techniques offers the ease of operation envisaged by H. G. Wells in his classic novel *The Time Machine*: "This lever, being pressed over, sends the machine gliding into the future," Wells's time traveler explains, "and this other reverses the motion." Whatever form time travel might conceivably take in some technologically advanced future, it certainly won't be as simple as that.

H. G. Wells
The author's fictional time machine was easy to operate — simpler even than boarding a train.

TIME AND GRAVITY

Ever since Albert Einstein published his general theory of relativity in 1916, scientists have assumed that gravity, the force that makes apples fall from trees and keeps the planets revolving around the sun, also has the power to warp time. As the force of gravity increases, time moves more slowly. Odd as it may seem, a clock in the basement of a building, where the earth's gravitational pull is stronger, actually goes more slowly than one in the attic — although the difference is barely measurable.

Scientists have visualized this effect by seeing spacetime — the three dimensions of space plus the fourth dimension of time — as a kind of rubber sheet. If you drop a heavy ball onto the rubber, the sheet will curve around it. This happens when the mass of a large body like a star exerts its gravitational force on spacetime: it bends all four dimensions into a curve.

Time loops

It is this effect that makes strong gravitational fields a possible opportunity for time travel. They might warp spacetime to such a degree that time would actually turn back upon itself, creating loops between past, present, and future. Sadly, such extreme gravity is likely to squeeze a would-be time traveler's body lengthwise like a strand of spaghetti.

FUTURISTIC FANTASIES

Time has long been at the mercy of writers' imaginations and twisted to meet the needs of their plots. In modern times a new genre of literature, known as science fiction, has been born from authors' attempts to chart the future.

O NE OF THE FIRST ATTEMPTS in fictional literature to describe the future is *Memoirs of the Twentieth Century*, written by Samuel Madden in 1733. This book is in the form of a collection of letters dated 1997 from British diplomats around the world to the Lord High Treasurer in London. It is more ambitious in concept than execution, and includes few imaginative insights into everyday life in the late 20th century.

Over a hundred years later, in 1843, Charles Dickens introduced the idea of time travel in *A Christmas Carol*. The leading character, Ebenezer Scrooge, travels into the future in the company of the Ghost of Christmas Yet to Come. Scrooge sees a vision of his own wretched death that persuades him to change his miserly ways. He turns over a new leaf and thus effectively changes the future.

The arrow of time

Dickens's tale is an imaginative treatment based on a conventional, linear view of time. Most people in the modern age see time as an arrow. We in the present are at the tip, and the past stretches back down the shaft. The present and past are fixed and immutable, but the future has no solid substance and is therefore open to influence.

Time travel within this framework presents some logical problems. If it is feasible to travel back into the past, the possibility arises that the traveler will influence events there, so changing the future — including the present he or she has just left. A story by Ray Bradbury entitled "A Sound of Thunder," published in 1952, is based on the idea of a company conducting "time safaris" into the past to hunt dinosaurs. Despite all precautions, one of the hunters accidentally steps on a butterfly, thus subtly but fundamentally changing the course of evolution.

Writers have tried different mechanisms for effecting time slips. Edgar Allan Poe's story "A Tale of the

Ragged Mountains," published in 1843, involves a man suddenly finding himself over 60 years in the past in the mountains of Virginia. The experience is vivid enough, but the reader is left to infer that it is a morphine-induced hallucination. *A Connecticut Yankee in King Arthur's Court* by Mark Twain, published in 1889, does not give an explanation of how the displacement in time occurred, but the

spiral spring. It was possible to travel directly from one turn to the next, and therefore to travel into the past or the future by an exact interval. The dramatist J. B. Priestley toyed with a similar theory in his play *Time and the Conways* (1937).

This theory of time as a helix is a development of the ancients' view of time as a cycle. The Mayans thought that the cycle was repeated every 52 years, while the Brahmans of India worked on a much longer time scale, estimated at 4,320,000,000 years. The rational, linear concept of time is a relatively modern invention, only widely accepted since the 17th century.

Even more modern is the concept of parallel universes and alternate worlds, introduced in the 1920's by J. W. Dunne, and since then eagerly exploited by sci-fi writers. English author Brian Aldiss sees alternate worlds as a sophisticated sub-genre of sci-fi, having its roots in history rather than science.

A fork in time

Steve Erickson's *Tours of the Black Clock* (1989) is an example of this increasingly popular sub-genre. The plot includes a fork in time that occurs at a crucial point during the Second World War. One strand of the story continues along the path of history with which we are familiar. The other strand has Hitler refraining from his attack on Russia, succeeding in his attack on Britain, and becoming locked in a war of attrition against the U.S.A., fought mainly in Central America.

Erickson's book also includes a reference to Albert Einstein's revolutionary work on the nature of time. Einstein's discovery at the start of the 20th century that time does not move at a fixed rate threw doubts on the linear concept of time previously accepted by the scientific establishment. Erickson's metaphor for this advance is that Einstein has wiped the numbers off the clock of time.

Therefore the 20th century becomes the last of all centuries, endlessly repeating itself in an eternal cycle of 100 years.

hero returns by falling asleep, suggesting that the whole experience may have been a dream.

Time as a helix

One of the most prolific sci-fi writers, Isaac Asimov, records that the first story he ever wrote was based on a revolutionary theory of time. "Cosmic Corkscrew," which was never published and has now been lost, posited the theory of time as a helix, that is, shaped like a

INDEX

Page numbers in **bold** type refer to illustrations and captions.

PHOTOGRAPHIC SOURCES

Ancient Art & Architecture Collection: 101bl, br; **Bryan & Cherry Alexander Photography**: 102t; **John Beckett**: 83t; **Bodleian Library**: 36, 49r, 58, 61l, 103l, 127b; **Bridgeman Art Library**: 20b, 21t, 22t, 23r, 33, 46t, 64t, 65, 68t, 96b, 97t; **British Library**: 41, 91t, 102b; Reproduced by courtesy of the Trustees of the **British Museum**: 34; **Jean-Loup Charmet**: 60t, 66-7, 67t, 106t, 108bl, 111c, bl; **Peter Clayton Associates**: 76c; **Bruce Coleman Ltd.**: 71c (K. Taylor); **John Cutten**: 82t; **Douglas Dickins**: 129cr; **C.M.Dixon**: 32t, b, 60b, 62b, 64b, 72t, 73t, 77tr, 86t, 128br; **Martin Eidemak**: 24-5t, 26; **Robert Estall Photographs**: 75tl (A. Fisher); **Mary Evans Picture Library**: 24b, 27c, b, 48t, 49l, 66l, 80b, 90t, 96t, 110bl, bc, 128tr, bl; **Werner Forman Archive**: 90b, 91b, 128tl, 129t, cl; **Fortean Picture Library**: 76tl; **FOT Library**: 110r; Marseille Tarot Deck made in France by **France Cartes**, 54138 Saint-Max Cedex, and supplied by **H.P. Gibson & Sons Ltd.**, London SW19 2RB: 112; **Giraudon**: 68b; **Susan Griggs Agency**: 74r (T. Spiegel); **Michael Holford**: 75tr, 97t; **Hulton Picture Company**: 50l, 51r, 72b, 77c, 82b (Bettmann Archive); **Hutchison Library**: 75b (J. Ryle); **Image Bank**: 57b (L.D. Gordon), 63 inset (F. Whitney), 124 (D. Landwehrle); **Images Colour Library**/Charles Walker Collection: 35, 37, 39b, 43, 48b, 53t, 86b, 101t, 106b, 110tl, 111tl, 122tr, br, 123r, 125r, 126tr, b, 127t, 129b; **Imperial War Museum**: 51l; **Kobal Collection**: 28t; **Frank Lane Picture Agency**: 63 (Silvestris); **Mail Newspaper PLC**: 52l; **Mansell Collection**: 90c, 137b; Courtesy of the **National Portrait Gallery**, London: 21b; **Octopus Publishing Group Ltd.**: 138t; **Popperfoto**: 50r, 52r, 69t, 73b, 81, 83b, 126tl, 132l, 139b; **Rex Features**: 12-13, 14l, r; **Ross & Cromarty District Council**: 61tr, br; **Scala**: 104-5, 107, 108tr, 109tl, tr, br; **Science Photo Library**: 8c (A. Bartel), 23l (Library of Congress/A. Johnson), 27t (A. Howarth), 28b (J. Baum), 30l & r (NASA), 31t (NASA), 40l & r (NASA), 47t (A. Bartel), 136t (S. Bensusen), b (Dr. R.F. Haynes, Molonglo Telescope, University of Sydney), 137t (Dr. J. Lorre), 138b (Royal Greenwich Observatory), 139t (T. Craddock); **Frank Spooner Pictures/Gamma**: 46b (Paris Observatory), 56bl (L. van der Stock), 59b, 69b; **Sygma**: 62t (J.L. Atlan), 80t; **David Towersey**: 87, 100, 108tl, bc, br, 109bl, 122l; **UPI/Bettmann**: 59t; Reproduced by permission of **U.S. Games Systems Inc.**: 111tr; Illustrations of the Hermit and Three of Swords cards from the Rider-Waite Tarot Deck reproduced by permission of **US Games Systems, Inc.**, Stamford, CT 06902, USA. Copyright 1971 by **US Games Systems, Inc.** Further reproduction prohibited: 111br; **Zefa**: 44 & 45 (K. Iwasaki), 56c (Photri), br.

TEXT SOURCES

We should like to thank the authors and publishers of the following books for allowing us to make use of their material in this volume:

The Prophecies of Nostradamus copyright © 1973 by Erika Cheetham and *The Further Prophecies of Nostradamus* copyright © 1985 by Erika Cheetham; extracts reprinted by permission of Perigee Books, a division of The Putnam Publishing Group. *Your Dreams and What They Mean* copyright © 1984 by Nerys Dee; extracts reproduced by permission of the Aquarian Press.

b - bottom; c - center; t - top;
r - right; l - left.

Efforts have been made to contact the holder of the copyright for each picture. In several cases these have been untraceable, for which we offer our apologies.